A NOTE ON THE AUTHORS

VICTOR GREGG was born in London in 1919 and joined the army in 1937, serving first in the Rifle Brigade in Palestine and North Africa, notably at the Battle of Alamein, and then with the Parachute Regiment, at the Battle of Arnhem. As a prisoner of war he survived the bombing of Dresden to be repatriated in 1946, and now lives in Winchester.

RICK STROUD is a writer and film director. He is the author of *The Book of the Moon*, *The Phantom Army of Alamein: The Men Who Hoodwinked Rommel* and *Kidnap in Crete: The True Story of the Abduction of a Nazi General*. He lives in London.

BY THE SAME AUTHORS

Rifleman
King's Cross Kid

SOLDIER, SPY

A Survivor's Tale

Victor Gregg
with
Rick Stroud

BLOOMSBURY
LONDON · OXFORD · NEW YORK · NEW DELHI · SYDNEY

Bloomsbury Paperbacks
An imprint of Bloomsbury Publishing Plc

50 Bedford Square   1385 Broadway
London   New York
WC1B 3DP   NY 10018
UK   USA

www.bloomsbury.com

BLOOMSBURY and the Diana logo are trademarks of Bloomsbury Publishing Plc

First published in Great Britain 2015
This paperback edition first published in 2016

British Library Cataloguing-in-Publication Data
A catalogue record for this book is available from the British Library.

ISBN: HB: 978-1-4088-6785-3
       PB: 978-1-4088-6786-0
     ePub: 978-1-4088-6787-7

2 4 6 8 10 9 7 5 3 1

Typeset by Newgen Knowledge Works (P) Ltd., Chennai, India
Printed and bound in Great Britain by CPI Group (UK) Ltd, Croydon CR0 4YY

To find out more about our authors and books visit www.bloomsbury.
com. Here you will find extracts, author interviews, details of
forthcoming events and the option to sign up for our newsletters.

This book is dedicated to the readers who have thanked me for writing about the world as it really is.

CONTENTS

EDITOR'S PREFACE

I met Vic Gregg nearly six years ago, just before his ninetieth birthday. Vic spent eight years of his life as a soldier and one of the many battlefields that he fought on was Alamein in North Africa. The purpose of that first visit was to ask him about the details of a soldier's life in the desert. I stayed far longer than intended and we talked for most of the day. Vic's wife, Bett, kindly made us endless cups of tea and plates of sandwiches. When we had finished I got ready to leave and, as an afterthought, Vic gave me a manuscript he had written for his grandchildren twenty years or so before – it was the story of his life. I showed it to my editor at Bloomsbury, Bill Swainson, who, after he had read it, agreed to take it on, and suggested that Vic and I collaborate to get the book ready for press.

A year later it was published as *Rifleman: A Front Line Life*. The book is mainly about Vic's time in the army, first in the Rifle Brigade and then as a member of the Parachute Regiment. One of the most vivid and harrowing parts of the story is Vic's description of the horrors he saw as a prisoner of war trapped in Dresden during the infamous bombing raid. Vic survived and when the planes flew home he spent the next five days helping to clear the thousands of burnt corpses of people who had been trapped in cellars and air raid shelters. Some of the bodies were unrecognisable as human beings. On the sixth day Vic escaped and eventually found his way back to England. Victor Gregg's time in Dresden was to resonate through his life and later his writing.

Rifleman was a success and with Bloomsbury's encouragement Vic went on to write in detail about his early life: a childhood spent growing up in the slums around King's Cross, London, and teenage years knocking about Soho. This next volume appeared as *King's Cross Kid.*

Bill then suggested that Vic write about his post-war life, which included undercover work for the Russians and working as a spy for British Intelligence, adventures that took him behind the Iron Curtain where he played a part in the fall of the Berlin Wall. Vic set to with gusto and the result is this book, *Soldier, Spy.* What started off as a story for Vic's grandchildren has ended up as a trilogy documenting some of the most momentous events of the twentieth century written from the point of view of a working man who played an important part in them.

Writing the three volumes has not been an easy ride for Vic and has sometimes been very painful. In the war he lost many close friends to the fighting. The Dresden experience left him with deep psychological scars, the mental damage that today we call Post Traumatic Stress Syndrome. Vic does not flinch from describing the man he became and the suffering he inflicted on his family. In a letter to me he wrote:

> *There were times during the writing that I had to face up to the fact of my inexplicable lack of conscience, my sudden spasms of inexcusable brutality to others and on the other hand my yearning*

*for the love and understanding of my family . . . During the last
six years I have attempted to analyse the two lives I have lived.
I can't accept that I could have been so cruel to those I loved and
yet I have been . . . I have arrived at the conclusion that I must
somehow have lived the life of two people, each totally different
from the other and for some reason unable to recognise each other
. . . What concerns me is why the better side of me failed to call
a halt to the darker side.*

The last five years have taken Vic on an intellectual and
creative adventure that would have astonished his fourteen-
year-old self, just out of school and starting to earn a living
doing odd jobs on the criminal fringes of Soho society. That
young boy met people that his older self described as:

*The arty-crafties, the weirdy-beardies, the folksy-wolksies
and every political creed under the sun . . . all earnestly discussing ways and means of putting the world to rights. {Soho,
Bloomsbury, King's Cross and Fitzrovia were the places} where I
learned the art of growing up.*

Now, seventy-five years later, Vic has become a writer and
mixes with the 'arty-crafties' and the 'weirdy-beardies' of the
publishing and media worlds. It has been my great privilege
to accompany Vic on this part of his journey and as we came
to the end of our work together he wrote to me saying:

*Thanks to yourself and the people who have been involved at
Bloomsbury I have been able to unburden myself from the ghosts
that have haunted me for the last sixty years and for that I thank
you all.*

As Vic's collaborator I know I speak for everyone who has worked with him when I say that this episode in the odyssey of Vic's life, and our work to bring his trilogy into the world, has been a fascinating experience, a very great pleasure and a real honour.

Rick Stroud
The London Library, June 2015

PROLOGUE

A Memory of Alamein

I remember one day during the Battle of Alamein when my friend Frankie Batt, a man I had enlisted with way back in 1937, was blown to pieces. I recall trying in vain to put the bits together, to somehow bring Frankie back to life. As I picked up what was left of him I could feel the hate burning inside me. Accounts would have to be settled. For the next three or four weeks our section of three carriers never brought a single prisoner back to the lines, despite the fact that the battle was nearly over and the enemy were coming forward in their hundreds with their arms raised in surrender. So long as no officer or senior non-comm. was witness we shot as many as we could until our anger died its own death.

Friends and well-wishers have told me over the years that I have nothing to feel guilty about and that me and my mates were only doing our duty. Even now, all these years later, I'm not so sure.

I fought in the Second World War from its start in 1939 to its fiery ending in May 1945 when I emerged from the ruins of the beautiful city of Dresden with my mind and body scarred. I witnessed things that I had not thought possible and my brain was filled with images of suffering that were to haunt me for the next forty years.

But for now the fighting was all over and the final gift from a grateful country was a civilian suit, a train ticket home and, if I remember correctly, about £100 of back-service pay.

Today we are called heroes but back then we got the impression that we returning servicemen were a necessary evil. For six years I had lived in a world where killing was both taught and encouraged. In this new post-war world it seemed to me that even a frown could get me in front of a magistrate on a charge of 'disturbing the peace'.

I had started out like all my comrades, soldiers, sailors and airmen, with a laugh and a song and finished up a prisoner of war in the ashes and rubble of Dresden, surrounded by pyres of burnt bodies. The events of the night of 13 February 1945 and the days that followed changed me more than anything that I had seen in all of the rest of the war. I thought that the people who were in charge, the masterminds behind the fire-bombing of the city, were tarred with the same evil brush as the enemy.

From that time onwards I felt I had to oppose authority whenever and wherever it raised its head. It was only after many years that I realised my anger had caused heartache and misery to those I loved while the forces that I struggled against carried on unrepentant and uncaring of the consequences. At least that is what I have come to think.

It is now more than seventy-five years since I set off from King's Cross in London, a brand new soldier boy keen to see what the Empire had to offer. What follows is not a history but a collection of memories by a man who has walked this earth for ninety-five years. I have tried to describe what happened to me in the brave new world that my mates and I had fought so long and hard for.

The NAAFI Canteen at Tregantle Castle, April 1946

There were about a dozen of us sitting round a battered canteen card table, and not a single one of us appeared to care whether we were winning or losing. Each of us had a fag dangling from our fingers or stuck between our lips. It was more like an eastern opium den than a military canteen; even the two girls sitting behind the NAAFI counter looked like they were from another world.

The sudden entry of the duty officer meant that something important was about to be announced. In he came, pinned a sheet of paper to the notice board and marched out as quickly as he had entered.

Somebody shouted: 'It's the bloody demob list, we're all out on 26 Group, 1 May, blimey that's next week.'

As if by magic the air of gloom and despondency disappeared, the girls started serving up beer and packets of Smith's crisps, the game was forgotten, the dog-eared cards slithering off the table and on to the floor. Nobody went to bed that night, Tregantle Castle would soon be history and to a man, whatever the rank, nobody regretted its passing.

Tregantle Fort, to give it its true name, was stuck on the very edge of the mist-covered vastness of Dartmoor. It was the arrival point for some of Britain's homecoming ex-prisoners of war, men who had been unlucky enough to have been banged up east of the Elbe. These were the prisoners who had been freed by the advancing Red Army and, since they had been tainted by contact with those awful Russians, the British government was taking no chances. There were about two hundred of us serving out the last few months of our service. We could be excused for thinking we had arrived at the infamous HM Prison, Dartmoor, which stood only a few miles away. For many of us the Fort was a monument to the lack of respect paid by a government to those men who had offered their lives to fight for their country.

For the next few days all the talk was about the return to civvy street, a thoroughfare that some of us knew nothing about. We had spent years being told what to do and what not to do, not knowing from one day to the next who would still be alive. Now we were going to be responsible for ourselves. In future it would be a case of earn a wage or sleep on the streets. But who cared? Let's throw these bloody uniforms in the bin, find a good-looking girl and shag ourselves to death every night.

The feeling was one of part excitement, part loss. It was like going into a strange town, where you knew nobody and where everything and every place was unfamiliar, just like walking through a minefield.

And so there we all were, formed up in lines, alphabetical order by surnames, in a huge corrugated-iron shed in this army depot in Plymouth. Inside it was bedlam. There were six lines of army-issue trestle tables, each line about a hundred yards long, taking up the entire length of the shed. The tables had large placards hanging above them, each showing four letters of the alphabet 'ABCD' 'EFGH' and so on. If your surname started with a 'G' like mine you went to the line that had a G. The tables themselves were piled high with clothes of different types and sizes, all organised with proper military precision. The first tables had the underwear, the socks and shoes. Then came shirts and ties and a pullover, all long-sleeved. Next came the suits and a selection of headwear. Finally, the recipient of all this free gear had the choice of picking an overcoat or a raincoat. Then you had to find a space near the wall where you could change and anything that didn't fit could be taken back down the line and exchanged. Along one wall, perched on a raised dais, was a military band doing its best to entertain us. Above all the noise we could hear the shouting of some non-comm: 'Come on you lot, the train's waiting, we ain't got all day.' The shed had been set near the station. You entered through the front doors wearing battledress and came out through the wide open sliding doors to the rear, dressed in civvies, straight on to the platform. We each carried a kitbag stuffed with our old army gear which we were told had to be kept in tip-top condition in case of an emergency recall. We were all now on 'Class Z Reserve' and liable for further call up if something happened.

The train had hardly left Plymouth when I pulled the carriage window wide open and pushed out the kitbag, feeling the tug of the wind as the train picked up speed. It began to slip from my grasp and then it was gone, carrying with it its redundant misery and evil memories. All the lads near me gave a roaring cheer as the bag and its contents disappeared. I was starting my life where it had been switched off all those years back. I was free, or so I thought.

That afternoon on Paddington Station I had a feeling that I was not ready for this sudden change. I remember having the idea in my head that if those around me were seeing things in white I would be seeing them in black. I felt a kind of fear, a strange sensation of not knowing what to do next. Out of the station and into Praed Street, and the first thing I saw was a couple of girls lolling against a brick wall, puffing away at their fags, as they waited for customers. I remember thinking, 'I wonder who's the big noise around here?' In my mind I was back in the dingy streets of Soho where I had spent my youth. The clock inside me seemed to be trying to make up its mind whether to go forward or return me to the past. Then I was on the Underground en route for the Caledonian Road and the haven of peace and eternal happiness that I knew I would find there.

I turn the corner into Ellington Street and climb the outside steps. The front door is wide open, as I had remembered it in the past, and I climb the stairs to the second floor. I look up, and there's my Freda gazing down at me.

At last I was back in the two rooms where Freda and I had started our married life after the battalion had been brought back from Italy to prepare for the second front, and we tied the knot. Freda had given birth soon after I had been captured at Arnhem. However, the face that confronted Freda now was not the same one that had returned from Italy more than a year earlier. During the fighting at Arnhem I had taken a blow to the face from a German rifle butt, half of my teeth had been smashed and the bruising, even after all these months, was still healing. There was no way I could be called a pretty sight. Freda never mentioned it but she must have been shocked at my appearance.

The infant I was now holding was the result of a week's leave, a never to be forgotten period of utter bliss. My little son Alan had been born into a world that was experiencing the death throes of the war. His tiny ears must have heard the crash of explosions and even through his closed eyelids he must have seen the flashes of light as the exploding V1s, or doodlebugs as they were called, sent him to the comfort and shelter of his mother's breast. That boy grew into a man but he never lost his love for his mother. He was always at Freda's side when she most needed support.

And so here we were, our little family at long last together. Love was going to be eternal and Freda and I were going to be eternal with it. And at first that's how things seemed to be turning out.

Like our parents and grandparents and most other people of our class we lived in two rooms, but we were happy; we could look the world in the eye without a shred of ill feeling. We were together and that was all that mattered.

Freda had a job with a big engineering firm right up in north London and it was her custom to take little Alan round to her mother's house in Collier Street first thing in the morning and then jump on a tram up to Tottenham and the factory. I knew I had to earn a living and find a job. I applied to the Post Office, a sure, safe bet with a pension at the end. I got the job easily enough but unfortunately I found myself unable to take orders from anyone I didn't know and trust. The Post Office job lasted less than six months and I was on the prowl again, looking for more lucrative work.

Freda had the idea that I should earn a trade.

'What about one of those government courses they keep advertising in the papers?'

I asked her, 'Who's going to keep you and Alan while we're existing on a fiver a week?'

'I can manage, Vic, and it won't be for ever. They only last six months according to what I read.'

'OK then, love, tonight we'll 'ave a stroll down to Collier Street and I can go and have a drink with your old dad.'

'Nana won't like it, dragging him out in the cold.'

'Don't be silly, cheer the old sod up.'

So that's what we did. We left our son in the care of Freda's mum who acted as his babysitter while we enjoyed a rare evening out with our friends. That night the pair of us sat in the local pub, chatting, laughing and joking. There was the usual lady playing the piano while somebody gave out a song. The door to the bar was wide open, the air laced with a combination of tobacco smoke, the overpowering scents of whisky, gin and of course the dozens of different aromas of the various beers that were available. It was a typical Saturday night repeated in any one of a million pubs up and down the land.

There were half a dozen of us crammed around the table — ourselves, a couple of the in-laws on Freda's side and another couple who had cheerfully made everybody tighten up as they jammed their seats into the small space. I had never set eyes on this couple before but it was obvious that they were part of the extended family.

What happened in the next few minutes only remains in my mind as a series of blurred movements. The tall and heavily built chap who, with his wife, had just sat down with us made a remark about Freda which caused some laughter among the others round the table. Freda looked uneasy. In a flash the man was being dragged across the table, all the glasses were sent flying and there I was, being hauled off the lad whose face was now covered in blood. I dimly remember that the whole pub had gone silent, bearing in mind that this was a family pub, everyone knew everyone else, but all that was known of me was that I was Freda's husband.

'Don'tcha know, 'e's just been demobbed, one of them para-troopers, bonkers if yer ask me.' As for Freda, 'What made you act like that, Vic? Showed me up proper, you did, what made you blow yer top like that, yer nearly killed him. Didn't you know that he is Cissie's old man's bruvver?' The answer to that one was that I didn't know and what's more I realised that what had registered in my mind as an insult and a threat was just Freda's mates joking and settling in for a good night out. This was not the only time I was violent, and the strange thing was that the incidents could occur without me ever realising the commotion that I had caused.

I apologised to all and sundry, but from then on I was treated with some caution. My Freda was waking up to the possibility that there might be something darker behind the shiny façade of the loving husband.

The most difficult part of my conversion from soldier to civvy was trying to be polite as people gossiped away about trivial bits of information that I considered not worth the time of day: 'Have you seen this film?' 'What about this, or that?' or chatting about something that I considered to be of no consequence. I must have been a right miserable sod, and I couldn't see it.

Thanks to Freda I had enrolled in a six-month decorating course at Hounslow. I was now qualified and earning a rea-sonably good screw working as a painter for whichever firm was paying the most money. Dozens of small contracting firms had sprung up all over London, fighting for the prize government and council contracts to repair the bomb dam-age that was everywhere. These firms did not have to put in estimates for the work, because the government and local council departments had a set payment per worker on the job. It was an invitation to the contractors to fiddle their way to making small fortunes. Each firm had a workforce of about two dozen men of all trades, but they would be drawing the wages for many more. When word came that an inspector was on his way to check up on the number of men on a site, the lads from the other sites would drop everything and rush round to make up the numbers. When he had made his tally and buggered off we strolled back to whatever site we had started on that morning.

Most firms charged the men out for an eleven-hour day, including Saturdays, but of course nobody worked those hours. I reckon that 90 per cent of the London building industry were in on the act. We had never had it so good.

If the bosses were on the fiddle so were we. If the guv'nor got a contract to repair a street of houses which were thought to be capable of repair, the five or six of us in the team would get to it, loading up a big handcart with all the gear and off we set. The job might be three, four or even five or six miles from the shop; there would be no lorry or van, not in those days. The handcart had to be pushed and pulled to the site and to make everything easy a stop was made at every coffee shop en route. Those working men's cafés were always called coffee shops, although nobody ever drank the stuff, the pre-ferred brew being a large mug of heavily stewed dark brown tea with a full complement of sugar followed by a couple of thick slices of bread and dripping, or maybe a huge bacon sandwich. The families that owned these eating houses knew exactly what their customers wanted and vied with each other to give it to them.

Arriving on the site, the first job was to find out the extent of the unofficial bonus we could make by rolling up any lead facing, along with any wiring which had a copper core, old lead water pipes and any other valuable scrap. Then we would pile it all on the cart and find the local scrap metal dealer. The next day the guv'nor would invariably ask how much we had fiddled, adding that so long as we didn't fiddle him, his eyes were shut. 'But don't expect me to bail any of you out if the law gets on to you . . .' That was the name of the game — you scratch my back and I'll scratch yours.

And that was how it was in those early post-war years. As for the incident in the pub, for the moment it was history but it was something that was going to happen again. I never knew what brought on these attacks and could never remember what had happened. Apart from that, it seemed that all I had to do was to slog away, earn a fortune and all would be sugar and spice.

2

The Daily Grind

Freda and I were now enjoying a life of bliss, and, except for a couple of brief interludes, I had settled down to a life of hard graft. We had moved away from Ellington Street and stayed for a few weeks with my mum in two rooms above her flat. Then Holborn Borough Council moved us into a nice two-bedroom requisitioned flat in Bedford Way.

This was part of a scheme to house the families that lived in the borough and whose men were home from the wars. The rooms were large and airy, we could look out of the window at the goings-on in Russell Square and, best of all, we now had a bathroom of our own. Freda lost the well-paid job at the engineering works in Tottenham when the firm decided to move up north, where it was rumoured that wages were half those in London. We didn't mind. Freda could have a nice rest and devote herself to mixing with the other new mums in the neighbourhood and I was earning more than enough to keep us well above the breadline. That's how it was in those days; we paid the rent and bought our weekly food in the local Co-op. There were no washing machines, no telly, no mobile phones; in fact, for most of us no phones at all, and of course no car. If we wanted anything that cost more than the norm there was always somebody who could 'put you in touch with a bloke I know', which, of course, meant that the purchase, which might be anything from a carpet to a complete suite of furniture, would accidentally fall off the back of a lorry. I haven't a clue how those people who lived in leafy suburbia managed: they always seemed to be complaining about the difficulty of 'making ends meet'. We never had that sort of trouble. If the local council or some landlord decided to up the rent everyone would be up in arms. A rent strike would be called by the local tenants' associations and talks entered into until a truce was called. An increase was judged fair if it was not more than a quarter of the original asking price.

Like all the other lads I found a lot of work pulling down old tenements or patching up those that were worth saving. Once an area had been earmarked for clearance then in moved the 'ball and chain', a gigantic concrete and iron ball that swung to and fro from a crane, sending anything in its path crashing to earth. Then the gangs of Irishmen arrived and in no time the site was levelled. All the building work was priced at so much per thousand bricks or so many square yards of plastering. We worked our guts out and, at 4s an hour, earned about £12 a week, a fortune in those days.

These big new council estates were replacing the rat-infested slum areas that blokes like myself had grown up in. 'Hey, Mabel, bring your old man up to our new flat, it's gorgeous, we got a barfroom and a lounge and three bedrooms, all for a quid a week' and in no time the locals would be clambering to get on the council lists. If you could prove that you had been bombed out of your home then you went straight to the top, otherwise it depended on the number of children you had.

Strangely, nobody wanted to take advantage of the London County Council's offer of moving a family, free of charge, to

any one of the new towns that were being built. It was the
women who complained the loudest: 'All my friends live
round here, if you fink I'm leaving them to live in some
snooty suburb you can fink again.'

The lounge and the three bedrooms had to be furnished.
The government began to ease the restrictions on hire purchase and the 'live now pay later' era started. The only bad
memories of those early post-war years were the nightmares
I experienced. Freda kept on at me to see a doctor about the
sleepless nights I was suffering, but I never let on about the
ferocity of the terrible visions that kept waking me up,
bathed in sweat. By and large I managed to keep submerged
the turmoil that was raging inside me.

3

Like Falling Off a Bike

In 1947 brother John was still out in the wilds of India serving with the Royal Artillery and I was using his bike to get to and from work. John's bike was a hand-built lightweight machine made by a certain Mr Hobbs who had his premises in the Barbican on the edge of the City of London. As a form of relaxation I had taken to doing small trips of a Sunday morning. One particular Sunday, a nice sunny June day, I was making my way back home along the old Epping Road, when who should I meet but one of the lads who I used to knock about with before the war, a chap by the name of Raymond. Ray had been excused war duty because he had been born with only three usable fingers on his left hand, but he was the only boy out of Kenton Street, where I lived, who could face up to the kids in the Wakefield and Harrison Street gangs.

Ray would tear into any boy rash enough to make snide remarks about his disfigurement. He also used to join me and my old mate Roscoe on our trips to the gym up at the Angel, although sensibly he refrained from taking part in the knockabouts that we enjoyed.

So we pull in at the next café and Ray's telling me all about life on the gravy train. 'You wasted ten years if you ask me, Vic. What made you enlist in the first place?' Even if I'd tried to explain I don't think Ray would have understood. Then Ray tells me that he belongs to a cycling club that's based in Barnet with about a dozen of the members who live in the King's Cross and Islington area. These lads rent out a room in Copenhagen Street which they use as a clubroom and have a training run every Wednesday evening. 'We have a forty-mile bash and end up in a pub just outside Barnet. Why not come along, Vic, see if you're as fit as you look?' From that moment I was hooked.

Ray was living with his mum and dad in a fairly respectable road off Finsbury Park; he peeled off as we were riding along Seven Sisters Road and I carried on to Freda and my boy Alan and a nice big Sunday dinner. No doubt about it, life was turning out well. The good wages that I was supplying kept the table loaded and Freda didn't have to worry too much about getting a job. I was working like a dog and that ensured that I had little time to dwell on the past. As we were sitting around that evening I mentioned meeting up with Ray and the forthcoming Wednesday night bash. Freda said, 'I should have thought that you were too tired to go out on a bike at that time of night. I bet it will be around eleven before you get home, you'll kill yourself.'

'Don't be soppy, Freda, I can do a run standing on my head, get some clean air down my lungs.'

The following Wednesday evening I'm mixed in with about a dozen other lads, all busy nattering away about nothing in particular. Then up comes Ray with a couple of his mates and introduces me to the crowd. I was riding brother John's hand-built Hobbs bike, which I thought gave me some clout. All Ray said was, 'If you want to still be with the rest of us when we reach the pub the sooner you put that load of overweight rubbish in the bin the better.'

'How far is this pub then?'

'We do a circular and finish up in Potter Street, have a pint or two and enjoy an easy ride home. All you have to do, Vic, is hang on for about thirty miles and try to get to the pub before we leave.' This caused some merriment among the others.

Then we're off and the column starts the grind up the Caledonian Road, along the Caley, past the Nag's Head, and in no time we're climbing up the gentle incline of the Archway Road and through Finchley. By the time Barnet Hill is reached the back markers are some half a mile to the rear and losing ground fast, and I'm beginning to hurt in parts I never knew existed – and there's at least another thirty miles to go.

The group travels northwards at a steady lick and I'm beginning to feel comfortable when I realise that coming up fast behind us is another gaggle of lads who sweep past us with the precision of a Swiss watch. They belong to the other half of the club who live in the Barnet area. There are now about thirty cyclists riding, heads down and in line ahead, catching up and passing the endless stream of overloaded heavy goods lorries starting their journeys to all points north of Watford.

We are going so fast that the number of lads able to keep up with the leading group drops fast. In the end there were twelve of us; then, with about a mile to go, four break away to arrive at the pub with about a minute to spare. Ray isn't one of the twelve! He arrives fifteen minutes behind and in a very sorry state. By that time I'm getting in with the twelve lads I had stuck it out with – nearly all of them are a few years younger than me.

'What club you riding with then, Vic?'

'I don't have a club, just came along for the ride.'

It turned out that this lot were only a small part of the Barnet Cycling Club. The main section sometimes rode out on a mid-week evening run but usually gathered for a Sunday ride of about fifty or sixty miles to a good-sized pub for a slap-up meal, then another trip to one of the many cafés deep in the country-side for a sit-down tea. This type of club run was very popular all over the country with everything arranged by the club's social committee. The racing teams of Barnet CC played a different part in the club's activities. They didn't really do the club runs; instead, they had two teams of six who did time trials and another small track group that raced at Paddington recreation ground every Thursday evening and on Saturdays at Herne Hill. Before we left the pub I agreed to do a twenty-five-mile time trial on the north London orbital course in three weeks' time. 'If we don't see you on Sunday, Vic, make sure you're here for the ride next Wednesday.' I think Ray saw me in a new light.

This was all new to me. The only previous experience I had of mixing with men who indulged in athletics was as a kid before the war when Bruce, the under-chef at the baker's shop where I worked, persuaded me to join him on his train-ing runs around the Inner Circle of Regent's Park. Those gentle sprints were nothing like the brutish methods used by these cyclists on their training runs. It was understood by all that if you had a problem nobody was going to wait for you – punctures, mechanical breakdowns, hard luck, those lads were out to win. They had no other topic but bikes, not foot-ball, cricket or rugby; it was all cycling and what tactics to use in order to crush the opposition.

Freda thought I'd lost my marbles, but I saw things differ-ently. I had found a way to express my desire to get to the top; all I had to do was to learn the ropes. The rest would be down to blood, sweat and tears and I knew all about that.

More importantly, I had found a way to let off the anger that I felt towards the world. Instead of blowing my top at people in authority I was now inflicting punishment on myself. For the first time since leaving the army there was a target to reach and every muscle in my body would have to work to help me reach the goal of winning everything in sight.

The following Wednesday I'm getting all sorts of advice. 'Vic, you're slogging your guts out for naught – if you want to beat the likes of us you've got to get some decent equipment. It must be like pushing a Tiger tank along the road with the bike and the wheels you're riding. This twenty-five-miler you're riding in next Sunday, it's a pure time trial. You're on your own starting at minute intervals; with that bike you won't do more than one hour and fifteen minutes, and that puts you at the bottom of the results sheet.' I was told that the winner would probably return a sixty-one-minute ride, or more if it was windy, perhaps sixty-two.

Trying to explain the order of battle to Freda the following Saturday evening was like talking to someone from Mars. As usual, we were sitting in the pub on the corner of Ellington Street supping up with the other family members, nearly all of them at least ten years older than me. Only Freda's sister Cissie and her old man were about the same age. Freda used to insist on going up to Ellington Street in Holloway, in spite of the fact that we were now living in Holborn. It wasn't a difficult journey: get the underground at Russell Square, change at King's Cross and get off at the station at Caledonian Road. The pub was a good ten minutes' walk from there. I told Freda that I needed to get a bit of shut-eye before ten as I had to be up at three in order to ride to the start of this event which began sharp at five thirty.

Freda didn't catch on straight away. Then, when it registered, she said, 'Are you telling me that you're going to rise and shine at three on a Sunday morning? Don't be daft, I'll believe that when I see it, now 'ave a sup up and behave yourself for once.'

The lonely ride before the crack of dawn, up to the Archway Tavern where I was going to meet up with the rest of the lads, was the first of many such rides over the next six years, a period of my life when I gave everything in the struggle to reach the top.

To everyone's amazement I finished that first time trial doing a short sixty-four minutes and finished in the top twenty. The half-dozen of us who had ridden in the event were on top of the world. Not only had we supplied the winner but also the team prize. Over the next few months Freda got used to my routine and the companionship of those young men with their one-track minds was just what I needed.

But there was a fly in the ointment, or to be more accurate, three flies. By now Freda had given birth to David, another fine boy, and there was no way she was going to stand for me doing the fifty or sixty miles a night that I was told was an essential part of the training routine. Her line was that 'being a proper father is more important than trying to be a superman'. She had a point. I got around the problem by finding work as a foreman on a big site halfway between Brighton and London. One hundred and ten miles round trip every day, three hours each way, rain or shine, and it paid off.

Ray used to turn up at our flat with what were called the 'start cards'. I'd sign and hand over the start fee and the club secretary did the rest. All I had to do was to be on the start line wherever the event was being held during the weekend and do the business.

The rest of the lads were now really getting on at me about my kit. 'Vic, you got to get a decent bike.' Easier said than done. Any bonus earnings I got were spoken for before I even opened my weekly pay packet. However, as was usually the case in my life, something turned up, this time in the form of one of the lads in the club who worked for a lightweight bike builder, Cyril, who had a shop in Penton Street, just a few doors down from the Angel Labour Exchange. Cyril was ex-RAF and had started the business with his demob money. 'Come up to the shop on Saturday morning, Vic, and have a word with Cyril.'

Cyril had a couple of frames hanging up in the window of his shop and I was not alone in admiring the craftsmanship of his work. I also knew that of all the bike builders in London he was probably the most expensive. A frame built by Cyril would set me back £12 to £14 minimum and then of course there were the wheels, not to mention the tyres, pedals and saddle. The list was endless. To get my hands on a suitable competitive machine I would be looking at some forty to fifty quid. In those days the average wage was about a fiver a week, maybe with some good bonuses seven or eight. Freda would never allow me to squander £50 on a bike; that sort of money would clothe the boys for a year.

Nevertheless, I turned up at the bike shop in Penton Street for the chat with Cyril. In no time we're reminiscing about our time in the army and the RAF. Then Cyril broached the subject.

'I've heard you need a bike, Vic, but you're short of the necessary.'

'You can say that again, Cyril, I could never afford your workmanship.'

'I hear that you're making a name for yourself with the boys from the Barnet?' He pointed to my bike. 'Is that the beast you're doing these times on?'

'Not even mine, Cyril, belongs to my brother John – the poor sod's still in India, won't be home till next year.'

'And you've been riding on those steel wheels? I notice you got down to sixty-two minutes last week in the Southern Counties ride.'

'Yeah, came in a close fifth.'

The lad who does all the brazing, the one who introduced me, brings in the tea, while Cyril has put his wife in charge of the shop. Then, 'What if I build the frame for free. For official purposes you have the frame on loan, but between the pair of us the frame is a gift. You pay for the enamelling and I will sell you whatever equipment you need at just over cost. The profit I make from the equipment will cover the cost of the material for the frame. You can spread the cost over the year, no contracts, just give your word.'

Cyril looked at me. 'What you reckon, Vic?'

'That's OK by me, Cyril, but what do you get out of the deal?'

'You're an amateur, Vic, I can't give you money to ride my bikes so what I do is to supply you with a bike that will set you alight, and every time you win the crowd will ogle this super bike with my name in the biggest type possible all along the down tube and on the head. In other words, I'm doing no more than that geyser down in Seven Sisters Road, Hetchins by name. He's sponsoring a whole team, you know them, you've raced against them.' The whole of the cycling world in southern England knew about these lads from up in Birmingham who rode in a team called the Monkton Wheelers. They were the current top dogs.

Cyril went on. 'The only thing I insist on is that the bike is always clean and presentable, as if it was in my shop window.'

'Goes without saying, Cyril.'

'If you're not racing tomorrow, Vic, pop in any time between ten and midday and we will measure you up. If you can do what David here says you're capable of then you will be like gold dust to me. I have to make at least one frame a week to keep going. It's not easy getting the lads to part with the cash.'

I turned up next day, a Saturday, not expecting anything great to happen.

'Let's get cracking then,' says Cyril. He dragged out what looked like an old broken bike frame, but in reality was a very cleverly constructed jig: all the tubes were adjustable. 'Just sit on the bike as if you were cruising along nice and steady.' Soon Cyril and his mate were shortening tubes, putting a bit more length in others and all the while I could sense that my whole posture on the bike was changing for the better. Next he went into angles, wheelbase measurements, bottom bracket height. Finally, Cyril nods his head. 'That's it, Vic, you're all measured up. When this job is done the bike will fit you like a glove. We should have it all brazed up by the end of the week, pick what saddle you want and start using it, get it nicely worn in. If you pay me a pound a week till what you owe is paid up that will be OK by me.'

'In that case I'm getting the best of the deal,' I replied, and we shook on it. Then the subject is changed and they're both asking me what it was like in the Paras, all the usual questions and I'm giving all the usual answers.

When I got home I tried to reassure Freda that no one was going to be the loser and she said, 'Since you've been doing the cycling you haven't been knocking all my friends senseless.' I put my arm around her and we were one again.

When I picked up the complete bike it was a stunner – enamelled in black with Cyril's trade name in inch-high lettering plastered along the main down tube and highlighted in gold. I was later told that the cost of the enamelling was more than the cost of the frame. Cyril had located a pair of Italian wheels and had got me four decent Dunlop tubs (tyres) from the Dunlop rep when he made his monthly visit to the shop. All in all he had saved me nearly twelve quid. I just couldn't wait to get the wheels rolling.

Freda did her nut when I explained that I would have to keep it in the bedroom. 'If I tear my stockings on your new toy it's going out of the window sharpish!' In the end I got my own way. 'Perhaps we can get a bigger flat off the council now we've got little David.'

The bike had its first taste of competitive racing in a couple of low-gear openers to the season. The low gear was 72 inches which meant that for every turn of the pedals the bike travelled 72 inches, achieved by a combination of wheel size, the number of teeth on the rear-wheel sprocket and the number of teeth on the chain wheel. It was generally reckoned that to have any chance of a win in the big Easter classics a low-gear time of sixty-two minutes over a course of twenty-five miles had to be achieved and that meant only one thing – buckets of blood, sweat and tears.

The first couple of low-gear events proved how much the quality of the bike mattered to a final performance. I turned in two sixty-three-minute rides, both of which were on very different courses, which showed how the terrain had little effect on the final result: up and down hills or on the flat made hardly any difference. My pedalling rhythm was constant at just under twenty-five mph; on a low gear of 72 inches that was reckoned to be as good as you could get. Now I looked forward to pounding into the dust anyone who stood in my way.

The leading light in the Barnet Club was a chap by the name of Alan Shorter, who, like me, found it difficult to bow and scrape to authority, especially the men who wore blazers and were the guardians of the National Cyclists' Union. These 'blazer men' controlled all the track and road events. It was them who had the final say about who was going to represent the country internationally. The majority of riders reckoned that Alan deserved a place on any national team, but Alan being Alan he refused to travel round the country at his own expense to ride in so-called qualification events. 'I'm either good enough or I ain't.' Alan never got selected.

Another thing that got the Barnet team into trouble was their refusal to wear the black tights and vests that were the dress code laid down by the Road Time Trials Council. The rule was a hangover from the very early days of cycling when the government banned all form of competition on public roads. The governing body in those days got around the rule by riding against the clock, not against each other. The riders started off at minute intervals and the fastest time won the day. To make the competitors as inconspicuous as possible it was decided that each rider would wear this black rigout. But that was eighty years ago and we rode in our multi-coloured vests and so regularly got banned as an example to the other clubs, although this didn't stop them from letting our lads on to their start cards.

In the late forties the year's racing calendar opened on Christmas Day with a low-gear twenty-five-miler. The drill was that the lads with the stomach to get out from between the sheets on a freezing cold morning at 5 a.m. cycled some twenty-odd miles to the start and then, once the event was over and done, off we went with a stop at the first pub that was open. The married men in the group usually got home at about four or five in the afternoon, just in time for their long-suffering wives to put the Christmas dinner on the table.

The really serious training started towards the end of February because we wanted to be in good shape to put the fear of God into the opposition when it came to the big classic races at Easter. On Good Friday the whole club converged on Herne Hill Cycle Track to support our track teams. These teams were made up of about twelve riders divided up between sprint and pursuit events. The competition at 'The Hill' was very strong, with the likes of Reg Harris dominating the sprint events and Cyril Cartwright winning the pursuit races. Reg was invalided out of the army in 1943 but even so, went on to fame and fortune on his bike, winning the world amateur sprint title in Paris in 1947. Cyril, of course, was the first man to finish the twenty-five-mile race in under one hour, and in 1950 took part in the Empire Games. With men like these two in the running, the only chance we had of a win or a place was in the individual pursuits and events like the five-mile 'Devil Take the Hindmost', an event that suited our lads down to the ground. At the end of a given number of laps the last man to cross the line drops out. This goes on until the last lap when the surviving bunch, usually about twenty-five riders, sprint for the finish. A right rough and tumble event, as far as I remember, and it was the only track event the Barnet riders ever had any success at. This didn't stop us giving them unstinting support in the other events even though we knew they didn't have a chance.

Easter Monday was a different story – nothing less than a win was acceptable and in order to achieve this we would have our spies out from February onwards trying to discover what the rival teams were up to. In 1948 the lads decided to enter the annual Actonia Cycle Club twenty-five-miler run on the Bath Road course. Provided there was no wind this was one of the fastest courses in the South of England and as the first man off usually went at about 5.30 a.m. the weather was generally pretty quiet.

This year the club had a team of four. We had no cars to take us to the event and very few of us could afford a bed and breakfast. So the usual drill was to rise from a fitful sleep at two in the morning, ride out into the freezing air, meet up with the rest of the gang and ride off to the assembly point which, in the case of the Bath Road event, was about forty-five to fifty miles away. On arrival we changed the road wheels for the much more expensive race wheels, which we took along bolted to a pair of lugs fixed to the spindle of the front wheel. Once the bike was ready we changed into our racing gear and stored our travelling clothes under a waterproof cape by the roadside. There might be more than a hundred competitors and we took up more than a mile of the verge.

After changing out of your warm clothing you had to wait with your teeth chattering and your extremities freezing

until your number was called. Then you cycled up to the line
to be held upright by a pusher-off. The timekeeper counted
down: 'Five, four, three, two, one', and then, with a shove
from the pusher-off, the torment of the next twenty-five
miles began. To do any good you had to have total concentra-
tion on the job in hand.

At that time in the morning there was little or no traffic,
so you could see the empty road stretching ahead. If you were
faster than the man who had started the minute before then
within two or three minutes you could see his black form in
the distance. The key thing was to keep up the rhythm you
had trained so hard to maintain. Trialling is all about self-
discipline, training and fitness. Clocks and watches fixed by
clips to the handlebars mean nothing: you judge your speed
by the rise and fall of the pedals. Within ten minutes your
body warms up, with blood pumped to every nook and
cranny. You forget the ice cold and fight the pain in the mus-
cles of your legs, arms and stomach as they adapt themselves
to this new regime of extreme action.

Depending on how fit you are the pain might last for the
next twenty or thirty minutes. For some riders it became so
unbearable that they couldn't take any more and were forced
to slow down. But the dedicated athlete, who only had one
objective, to win at all costs, rode through the pain until his
body accepted a new world where speed was everything.
Whatever the road did, however it twisted and turned or rose
and fell, every ounce of energy had to be used to maximum
effect; once you were on the bike that was it, only the legs
moved, the body, arms and head staying as still as possible.
Towards the end of the first fifty minutes the body was
screaming to stop, every muscle crying out for release, the
eyes blinded by sweat, the road ahead a blur and all feeling

dominated by the agony of air being forced into the lungs, which were gulping for oxygen while the mind applied maximum power to the legs.

A twenty-five-mile time trial was the one where the rider took the most punishment as he hurtled flat out for sixty-one minutes or less. George Fell was the lad who broke the sixty-minute record with a short fifty-nine-minute ride (short meant under fifty-nine minutes and twenty seconds; long meant over that and under sixty minutes). Over the next few years the record came down to about forty-nine minutes.

The course took us from Pangbourne Lane on to the Bath Road, through Newbury and up towards Marlborough. At twelve and a half miles you turn for home. Fastest time wins.

I started the event with a handicap of one minute and twenty seconds. I recorded a time of sixty-two minutes and five seconds in a morning of hailstones and gale-force winds to win with a twenty-five-second advantage over the second best time. The bike had proved itself. I also collected the handicap prize and the Barnet Club had the satisfaction of taking the team prize.

The bugbear was that this was an amateur event so I didn't actually get any cash. The prize was a chit which you gave to your local bike dealer in exchange for goods or cash. This was the way of getting round the amateur rules forbidding financial rewards, but it was not much good to Freda whose only interest as far as the bike was concerned was how I was going to pay for it. 'Not by cutting my money, I hope.'

One way and another my winnings amounted to a chit for £5 which, in exchange with the dealer, would come out at about £3 10s cash. I handed the lot over to Cyril who in return gave me the full £5 off what I owed him for the bike.

So, bit by bit, over the months I paid for the bike. The frame had been built for track and road events so I was able to compete in both. Cyril said I was like a gold mine to his business.

Meanwhile, some of us who were slightly older became aware of a new youngster, Ted Gerrard, who had joined the club ranks before reaching his fifteenth birthday. He was unstoppable. It took him a brief eighteen months of mediocre times and then one bright day he entered a time trial organised by the RAF of all people and came home with a middle fifty-nine minutes, the fastest time ever recorded by a club member. Young Ted was now *numero uno*, and that gave me a jolt. And he wasn't the only competition. Five weeks later on the Southend Road I recorded my first under-the-hour ride. Not that it did me any good – the invincible George Fell took the event with a fifty-nine minutes and five seconds. I eventually came fourth. Just when I thought I had finally made it to the top, down come the times all round. Back to the drawing board.

When Ted got called up for national service and went into the RAF we older and slower members heaved a sigh of relief, but not for long. The champion cyclist and frame-maker Alan Shorter, ever on the lookout for fresh talent, took a prodigy under his wing, a young lad by the name of Alf Engers. So much faith did Alan have in this young man that he lent the money to have a bike specially made for him and young Alf soon paid for it with bonus after bonus. A few years later, when I had disappeared from the scene, Alf became national champion three years on the bash and to peak everything he got the twenty-five-mile time down to forty-nine minutes. Along the way he fell into trouble with the authorities and for a while lost his amateur status. But

Alf was the king, that's how he was known the length and breadth of the British cycling scene – 'The King'. Two other members of the club I still remember, Jack Styles and Ken Brewer. I must have had some relationship with these lads but, dig as I might, why their names are still in my memory bank is beyond me. We must have had some fun together.

It was in the first major classic of 1949 that I made my acquaintance with another aspiring champion, a chap by the name of Dave Keeler. Dave was a member of the Vegetarian Cycling & Athletic Club and was always saying that he won his races on a diet of dates and plums. True or false, Dave was fast and he was to be my shadow for the next five or so years. Dave had the advantage over me because he was eight years younger; other than that it was a see-saw rivalry which included our competing for inclusion in the British cycling team for the 1950 Commonwealth Games in New Zealand. The event was the 4000-metre solo pursuit. At first I had the edge over Dave when I came home first in another rain-soaked time trial on the undulating course up at Bishop's Stortford. But Dave came right back at the Easter meeting at Herne Hill, beating me by some eight seconds in a deciding 4000-metre pursuit.

In cycling circles around London I was getting noticed. The bike Cyril had built for me ran like oiled silk. He had got the measurements exactly right, and I just sat and pedalled – quite different from what I had experienced on John's bike. The new bike made it all seem so easy; what wasn't so easy was the fact that the lads I was competing against were usually five years my junior. I found a lot of satisfaction in winning and proving that I was better than the rest, but the lads I beat were prepared to sweat blood to get their own back and give me my comeuppance. If I showed the slightest weakness or lack of fitness those young bloods of twenty-five would jump in to snatch the laurels. And, of course, having climbed almost to the top there was no way that I was going to go down without a fight.

I wasn't doing this for the fun of it. It was a way of asserting myself against anyone standing, with the advantage (to them) that I didn't have to come to blows to do it. All the bodily pain was being inflicted upon myself, by myself. Winning was the be all and end all. Any other consideration, including my duties as a husband and father, became invisible as my vision became more and more blinkered. I learned, too late, that to reach the top in any profession it's necessary to have a one-track mind. If you're going to take on other responsibilities then ditch the thought of ever trying to get to the top or, better still, get to the top first, then once you've satisfied your ego you can indulge in the luxury of marriage. And that is how it was. I hardly noticed that I was doing a first-class demolition job on my relationship with Freda.

Any woman worth her salt puts one objective above all others: the wellbeing of her brood. This is something that's built into them, and as they see things the father has to play his part. As a father the most important job next to supplying the wherewithal to feed, clothe and house the family is to commune with the kids, take them up the park of a Sunday morning while the little wife gets on with the chores like cooking the Sunday roast. Then, in the evening, I'm supposed to take the kids up to their beds and read stories that will bring sweet dreams to their cherubic little faces.

What I am *not* supposed to be engaged in is filling the house with the evil smell of Goddards Embrocation in the summer or a mixture of wintergreen and olive oil in the winter. I'm not supposed to live on a racing diet of brown bread and pressed dates. I'm not supposed to come home in the evening from work and, after snatching a meal, go out and start charging up and down the roads of Middlesex, Surrey or Kent chasing some impossible dream. Freda said to me, 'You're a grown man now, not some teenager. Don't you understand that you have responsibilities? The kids only see you when you're too knackered to know that they're there.' It all fell on deaf ears. I had developed a one-track mind I don't think any of my family and friends approved of. More so as Freda had a quality about her that attracted all comers. As well as thinking about me as being a right sod, my family and friends may well have questioned my mental state, and I couldn't see it. I was blind as a bat, oblivious to the harm I was doing.

I finally said my goodbyes to my mates in the Barnet Club when they decided to go over to mass-start road events like the annual Milk Race. I could not get used to the team work necessary for this side of the sport. If I was going to win then it would be by my own efforts and not by taking a back wheel and then coming out and trying to outsprint the rest of the bunch to the line. Anyway, I was useless as a sprinter and I knew it.

I decided to have one last go and joined the Polytechnic Club. Their clubroom was in Upper Regent Street in the Polytechnic building. I had two reasons for switching allegiances, the main one being that I was doing a lot of road training with a couple of the lads from the Club; the other was historical. I knew that the Polytechnic Club, or at least the athletic part of the Club, was the result of the philanthropic actions of the father of one of the senior officers of my old Regiment, Quentin Hogg, and this fact drew me like a magnet. The change did me little good because I failed to recognise the obvious, that I was past my best. True, I could still produce the times, but those extra seconds which meant the difference between winning and losing were now getting further and further from my reach. Blinded by ambition and ego I refused to admit defeat.

My departure from the sport was caused by a crash in the North Middlesex and Hertfordshire 'Hundred', a classic race in the north London time-trial calendar. Cyril had made me a handlebar extension that I could modify according to the nature of the course I was competing on. It had a floating lug so that I could move the handlebars backwards or forwards. For the 'Hundred' I put the bars another half-inch further forward than usual, tightened the lug and sawed off the end of the extension. That was it, super, just the job. I had trained hard for this event and was now riding for the Poly who wanted to put the Barnet and any other clubs who thought that they ought to be top dogs in their rightful place – right down at the bottom of the ladder.

The weather was perfect when we started, not warm but dry and crisp and gradually getting warmer. As I crunched out the miles I could feel my fitness kicking in. By halfway I was two minutes up on the next man. I didn't feel the need to pressure myself, just keep the pace going. The checkpoint at Girtford Bridge had come and gone and I was now on the last thirty-mile circle around St Neots, just north of Biggleswade. I altered my position to keep the rhythm going and without warning the handlebars slid off the stem, throwing me head first into a ditch. Luckily the bike carried on and came to rest without my weight on it. As I lay there I could feel the pain coming from my right shoulder. I climbed out of the ditch, fixed the bars the best I could and started the long ride home. I finally made it to University Hospital in Gower Street where the doctor, after a quick examination and a clean-up, left me with the words, 'Don't fret, son, it's probably only a sprain, be better in a couple of days.' Three days later I reported back and they decided to X-ray the shoulder joint. It had come adrift. 'We can replace it and pin it which means you will be in a plaster cast for about ten weeks, although I must tell you there is no guarantee that the bones won't spring apart again, or you can leave it and it will repair itself, although the joint will never close up. The worst you'll get is a touch of rheumatism in damp weather'. To this day I have the bump in my right shoulder where one bone is higher than the rest.

The crash put me out of competition racing for six months, by which time I was quite unable to reproduce the form that I had built up at so much cost. I could manage a third or maybe fourth in the average run-of-the-mill event but that was useless to me. Coming second was a no go, so I thought if you cannot win, get out. Which is what I did.

In all I put in six years of concentrated effort. I was constantly kidding myself that in spite of my age and the responsibility of bringing up a family I could reach the top. Encouraged by my occasional wins and the fact that whatever event I entered I never finished lower than seventh or eighth, I had started each event expecting to shatter the opposition. It didn't happen, so what? I'll try a bit harder next time.

The best part of the joke is that, search my mind as I may, I can never remember a time when I could honestly say that I enjoyed cycling. To me it was a means to an end; my satisfaction came from the amount of punishment I could take while satisfying my urge to destroy the opposition.

Those six years were the only period of my life after my demobilisation when I was free of the torments that hounded me in my later years. During those years of intense struggle there was no time for thinking or brooding on the past; I was too taken up with my will to win and to beat the opposition.

I have often wondered why I kept at it. I think something that happened in the war prepared me to keep on slogging away. We were about to fight the Italians at Sidi Barrani, halfway between Mersa and the border with Italian-ruled Libya, and our commanding officer decided to give us a pep talk. 'Men,' he called out in his best parade-ground voice, 'tomorrow morning we're going to give them a prod up their backside, with luck, we might even do them some damage. Whatever happens I want you all to understand that this war is probably going to last at least for the next ten years. In the end we will be victorious, but it isn't going to happen tomorrow, or the next day, or even next year.' He made us all recognise what we were up against, and that we were in for a long march. That little speech was still helping me. So I didn't win today, and I may well not win tomorrow, but I was certain that in the end I would reach my objective. That was something I always believed. For the first time in my life I was living on a planet of my own choosing. With my tunnel vision I could home in on a target of my own choosing, but that same tunnel vision failed to highlight what I was doing to my family.

As it turned out I threw in the towel just in time. The marriage managed to get back on an even keel. Freda's line was: 'So you're not the big noise that you wanted to be, so what? You're not like a load of your mates who come home from work and then disappear from the family to go down the pub. At least you've decided on your own to pack it all up. All you got to do now is to get a nice steady job and spend the evening with me and the kids and we'll all be in heaven.'

Within a month of jacking it all in I gave the bike to a youngster who I knew was as keen as mustard but never had the wherewithal to get the kit he wanted. As for me, my battle cry was: never look back, never say die, start a new road, and get cracking.

4

Back to Normal

Alongside all the competitions and training I had to earn a living. In 1949, my third year of freedom from the army, I was trying to find work that would leave me enough time to train. One of the lads I knew thought that he could get me into one of London's really high-class painting firms. He was making a start with them himself the following Monday. 'Come along with me, Vic, and I'll get you in.' That's how I started work with Hamptons of Pall Mall, probably the most prestigious building firm in London. The pay was well above average, the work was in large houses, government offices along Whitehall, Buckingham Palace and the major hotels in the West End. The standard of work was higher than average and we had to make sure that our whites were clean and tidy.

I stuck it with Hamptons for almost a year, by which time I had been put in charge of the jobs that needed a small crew of lads who were good at ladder work. The money was reasonable, and I was home by six almost every evening.

One day, when I was working on the outside of the first-floor windows of the Wallace Collection in Manchester Square, I became aware of a man calling up to me from the pavement. I looked down at him and thought he seemed vaguely familiar and looked as though he had just left the exhibitions. I recognised him as 'Dixie' Deane, a paratrooper who I had dropped with into the battle round the city of Arnhem. In no time I was down at ground level and there we were shaking hands and chatting away nineteen to the dozen. He told me that he had looked up and recognised me in a flash. I told the lads I was going for a cup of tea at the Express Dairy café just round the corner and Dixie and I trotted off.

Dixie told me what happened after the support section, of which I was a part, had been separated from the battalion line. The two Vickers heavy machine guns and one of the pair of three-inch mortars had been detailed to site themselves on the south-western corner of the largest of the three drop zones. Our Colonel then marched the remainder of the men off in the general direction of the main objective, the bridge at Arnhem. Dixie couldn't remember what happened that first night except that they were continually on the move trying to find a way around the enemy tanks that had appeared. He told me how the battalion was being torn to pieces by this armour. Halfway through the day Dixie received a bullet in the eye, his position was overrun and by sheer luck he was taken to a Dutch hospital. He was given a blood transfusion, the donor being a German soldier who had the same blood group as Dixie. That same afternoon the bloody engagement ended with the destruction of the remainder of the battalion. 10 Para had lasted two days. By the end of the second day, of nearly four hundred men who made the jump only eighty of us were left standing. We parted with the usual promises to meet again but, alas, we never did.

I can't remember why I left my job with Hamptons, but I transferred my allegiance to a dodgy firm who were pay-ing enormous wages to get idiots like me to work on a

street of bombed-out rubbish up behind Chapel Street in
the Edgware Road.

It was around the corner from this job, at Marble Arch,
that I bumped into an ex-Rifleman, Charlie Forbes, who had
been with me in Dickie Bird's carrier platoon in the desert in
1942. After the usual greetings the talk turned to work.
Charlie asked me, 'What you working on then, Vic?' 'The
usual stuff, mainly bomb damage, pays well if nothing else.'
'I can get you a real good start if you want,' says Charlie. He
goes on to tell me that he can get me into the best painting
contractor in south London.

'We've made a start on the South Bank exhibition site and
the guv'nor's on the lookout for lads who can take the weather.
Know anything about spray work, Vic?' to which I reply in
the affirmative. 'That's it then. Give that potty lot you're
working for a drop kick and make your way down to Battersea
Park. I'm a foreman there. Take it from me, you'll be earning
a bomb. Make sure you bring your ticket with you.'

'Ticket! What ticket?'

'Ain't you a union member then, Vic?'

'Never given it a thought,' says I. Charlie explained that if
a man wanted to work on these sites he had to be in the
union: no ticket, no job. 'Get yerself up to Grafton Way, it's
off the top end of Tottenham Court Road, and they will send
you to the nearest branch. Take it from me, it's worth the
trouble.' With that Charlie was on his way, doubtless to earn
some of them bombs he was talking about.

Four years had gone by since I was demobbed and my conversion from warrior to work addict had not gone smoothly.
The local employment exchange in Penton Street had given
me up as unemployable, because I wouldn't take orders from
foremen and the like.

The job we were working on in the Edgware Read was a real fleapit, pulling down the old lime and plaster walls and ceilings which meant that all and sundry got coated in a layer of dust and filth. There was a new danger about which we knew nothing: asbestos. The new plasterboard that was being used contained lots of it. Unaware of the danger, we cut the stuff, sawed it into shape and with no washing facilities available sat down at our meal breaks smothered in it, merrily chewing our way through whatever the wives had put in our lunch bags. There was no way I could go home in the filthy state I used to get in after a day on this particular job, so I had made it a practice of having a bath at the public baths in the Caledonian Road before going home. When I eventually got back the two boys always came running up to their dad and I always got a loving kiss from my beloved Freda. That's how it was. I was as happy in those years as I was ever to be in the future.

The next morning, following Charlie's advice, I took time off the job and whipped round to the union offices in Grafton Way, off the Tottenham Court Road, a small two-roomed office up on the top floor. The door's open so I go straight in and explain to the bloke sitting at the only desk that I wish to sign on for a ticket. He takes my particulars, writes out the time and place where I will have to present myself. Then he stands up, holds out his hand and says, 'Tidy yourself up before you go: they're a bit critical, that King's Cross Branch.' He told me to attend the next meeting of the branch which was to be held as usual in the assembly rooms of a large pub off the Caledonian Road. 'And good luck, mate.' With the note of introduction safely tucked away, I went back to the Edgware Road to carry on where I had left off the day before.

On the evening of the branch meeting, wearing my best and only suit (the one given gratis by our grateful government), I turned up at this big pub near Pentonville prison in the Caledonian Road. I introduced myself to some of the men during the drinking session before the meeting started and any qualms I had about my reception as a 'newcomer' disappeared. The big upstairs room was full, and the noisy chattering came to an abrupt halt when a man sitting at the main table to the front of the hall banged this big wooden hammer on to the block of wood. 'This meeting is now in progress. Any strangers leave the room until called.' Then I and another couple of potential members were ushered out and told to be prepared for up to an hour's wait. 'Go downstairs and have a sup while you're waiting but don't get pissed, you will have to answer questions.'

In due course the same lad came down and escorted us back up to the packed room. Another man handed a sheaf of papers over to the bloke at the table, bang goes the hammer, he announces my name and I go to the front of the class and prepare for a verbal onslaught. Why did I want to join the union? How would I do this, or that? Did I know the difference between linseed and boiled oil? And so on. When it was over the hammer man asked for a proposer and a seconder. I didn't have a clue what he was talking about but I got my proposer and seconder. The meeting was asked to vote for me, up went a show of hands. 'Anyone against.' Not a single hand rose in the air and the next thing is that I am now a member of the King's Cross Branch of the National Society of House and Ship Painters.

I was given a book of instructions on how to conduct myself. Never disgrace the union and long live the Queen. I was to present myself in Grafton Way the next morning to collect my ticket. Presumably I would then be in possession of the key to perpetual wealth. When I finally arrived back home Freda greeted me with, 'Let's hope they get you a job so that you don't have to bring all that dirt and filth back any more.'

The next day I went down to the Festival Gardens at Battersea Park, right by the Thames. The first thing I noticed was that nobody was working, just lounging about and chatting. When I found Charlie he said, 'Not to worry, Vic, just 'aving a little stoppage that's all, be settled in a couple of hours.' The site had stopped work over the issue of wellington boots. The trouble with the site was – that is until the groundworkers laid the hard core and had tarmacked the surface – the whole area would regularly flood, because as the tide came in the river flowed in under the embankment, turning the whole place into a sea of mud.

Sure enough, round about ten in the morning a big wagon drew on to the site with boxes full of wellington boots of all sizes. 'Don't we 'ave to pay for them then, Charlie?' 'Not on your life, Vic, they want the work done they pay for the wellingtons, that's what you're paying your union dues for.'

One day on the site an odd thing happened. The gang of Irish lads who were doing the groundwork were in the process of levelling the two-foot-thick layer of hardcore on an area in the centre of the site. The lads were raking away while following them was a massive steamroller with its huge front roller flattening everything before it. Like any steam train this enormous beast was managed by a driver and the fireman, whose job it was to keep the fire going by constantly shovelling coal into the boiler opening. The men who witnessed what happened next were transfixed to the spot as the steamroller suddenly began to sink into the ground, accompanied by a loud sucking noise. It finally came to rest with the smoke still belching out from the funnel and the two terrified crewmen clinging on to the rope attached to this funnel. To this day the machine lies buried under the grass of Battersea Park. It was too heavy to retrieve.

The time for the opening of the Festival Gardens grew nearer and the bonuses came thick and fast. The job lasted until the first week in May 1951, when the site was officially opened. It certainly had been a good earner.

It was while I was working at the park that I learned about the politics of these union-controlled building sites. The man who was really the head boy was not one of the big contractor's clerk of works or some strong-arm foreman; no, the boy in charge was the chief Federation Steward. The Building Trades Federation was an organisation that served as a central control over all the different unions on a site. There would be a daily site meeting chaired by the Federation Steward which all the reps of the different unions attended. Issues were debated and by a simple show of hands a remedy found which kept the lads earning the big pay packets. This doesn't happen today because almost all the smaller and medium-sized craft unions have been swallowed up by the big boys. Right up to the mid-seventies any large building site could have as many as fifteen to twenty craft and general labouring unions, each one defending its work practices against the others. The electricians would down tools immediately upon hearing that some chippy belonging to the woodworkers' union had fixed a light bulb, the rule being 'one man, one trade'. While the employers were making their huge profits they seemed quite happy about the unions running the job. The unions' aim was to keep their members working and at the same time wring as many bonuses as they could out of the system. So both sides were on to a good thing. What we saw at the Battersea Park site was that if any employer caused waves that might rock the boat, the other employers would step in and tell the offending contractor to ease off.

It was during the time of my working at Battersea that the British government made a payment of £80 million to the German government to help them get on their feet after the war. Not many of us had a problem with that, until it emerged that the money was going direct to the huge German consortium headed by the Krupp company. The godfather of this vast organisation had been convicted at Nuremburg as a war criminal and had recently been released. Surely this couldn't be true, I thought. The only newspaper that stood up against this was the Communist *Daily Worker*, which to all intents and purposes was the site newspaper. The *Daily Herald*, which in those days was the official voice of the Labour Party, trumpeted that bygones should be bygones. Before the week was out I had contacted the site Communist Party branch and offered my services.

5

Card-carrying Member

My application for membership at the Festival site branch of the Communist Party eventually led to an invitation to attend a meeting of the Holborn branch in Holborn Hall, a building opposite the Gray's Inn Road police station.

It took me exactly thirty minutes to blot my copybook. On the agenda was a discussion about some pamphlet from the brain of the big white chief, Uncle Joe Stalin. I sat at the back of the room hardly able to believe that these people were taking all this mumbo-jumbo seriously. All of a sudden I realise that I'm being addressed by the chap who's in charge of the meeting.

'Have you arrived at any conclusions, comrade? What do you think?'

'Yes, tell us what you think?'

'Do you mean that you lot believe all that crap about the struggling working class?' I said. Deathly silence all round the room.

I learned a lesson on that first evening. Most people will sit in silence, even when they are listening to a policy they don't believe in. From then on I had a new vocation: I became a sort of devil's advocate, an obstructive sod who would agree to nothing unless I was absolutely convinced that it was correct.

Following my sudden leap into working-class politics it didn't take me long to size up the political leanings of the committee of the King's Cross Branch of the National Society of House and Ship Painters: 100 per cent Communist Party membership. I was immediately made minutes secretary, fair and square, proposed, seconded, voted in unanimously. 'Right, Brother Gregg, all you have to do is to sit at the table and jot down every word that is said in the course of the night's business. A true record is a very important thing.' I was now on the committee of one of the most militant left-wing trade union branches in the London area, and I hadn't lifted a finger. The next step up the ladder was when I was told that from now on I was to forget those potty members in the Holborn Branch. I was now part of the industrial section of the Party. 'Confidentially, Vic, Uncle Joe can spout as much as he wants, we have only one policy – keep the lads earning and shut out all the lightweights. By 'lightweights' he meant the men who came from outside London, with no card, trying to undercut everyone's wages. The Party card was a signal, not of our allegiance to Moscow, but of our resistance to capitalist evil, represented by the Conservative and Unionist Party of Great Britain. But, remember, I was not a pacifist. If the Russian government had at any time attempted to take over Britain I would have joined up again and fought without a second thought.

To be an active member of the Communist Party in those early Cold War days it was necessary to have the hide of a rhinoceros to resist the combined weight of the national press and the BBC. During the meal breaks in the factory canteen out would come a copy of any one of the big dailies, the pages would be turned to the comics or the sports page, and almost to a man the headlines were ignored. If by chance

Arsenal were playing Spurs on the same day as an election then it was the game that got the attention.

By 1951 the Battersea Park job was a thing of the past, and the great British public were now enjoying the fruits of the hellish conditions the workforce at Battersea Park had suffered under. Then one day the union branch secretary said, 'Vic, if you're willing to get to Borehamwood we can get you started up there and you'll have to bring your wages home in a suitcase.'

The Borehamwood job suited me down to the ground. The twenty-mile ride up to the site was a good training ride and fifty miles a day was enough to keep me fit and ready for the weekend. An added plus was that I could be home and dry by seven in the evening which meant that Freda and the kids would be happy.

Living as I did almost next door to the Party printing house in Farringdon Road, it was my job to see to it that the Party paper, the *Daily Worker*, was available on site. This was considered to be most important: the number of men on the site was about four hundred and we were expected to sell forty or fifty copies of the paper every day. The main weapon on site was a big notice board measuring about ten feet by twelve. It had news of all the big sites in and around the Home Counties. Part of the job of the Federation Steward was to forward to central office a report on site conditions, work available, possible earnings and all the general news and information thought to be useful to the workforce. Down in the corner of the board was a sentence telling all and sundry that the board was the property of the Communist Party of Great Britain and, as a finishing touch, pinned up on the side was that day's copy of the *Daily Worker*. The board also gave news of any chicanery the employers were getting up to.

The Borehamwood site was a brand new government housing project north of Barnet. The following Monday I left home at 6.30 on a bright sunny morning and reported to the site steward who then directed me to a painting firm where, after completing only a week's work, I was elected as the union rep with responsibility over about two hundred painters. The simple reason they voted for me was that all they wanted to do was work their arses off and earn fistfuls of money.

My first lesson about the opposition to organised labour came when the union reps on site were called to a meeting by the Federation Steward. He had been called to the offices of the main contractor to see if anything could be done about a contingent of rogue Irishmen who were causing trouble with the regular Irish employees. The firm was at a loss as to how to deal with the matter. The invading troublemakers were led by a priest who was going around waving a huge Holy Bible.

The Catholic Church did not like the Communist Party and they used their influence on the Irish lads who were flocking to Britain, drawn by the prospect of jobs for unskilled labour. There was no problem with the Irish workers who were already in the system. They were almost all union card holders. It was the new arrivals who were the problem. The Church paid their fare across the Irish Sea and arranged their lodgings, warning them that they were to keep away from the unions, telling them they were all controlled by the Communists who, as everyone knew, were the avowed enemies of his Holiness the Pope and the Holy Virgin.

We told the firm not to worry – the site committee would deal with it pretty quickly. The union reps thought that these Irish Fusiliers should be left to fight their own battles.

The term Fusiliers referred to a well-known Irish ballad
called 'McAlpine's Fusiliers'. It was quickly pointed out by
the Fed Steward that if the Irish lads didn't dig the holes no
new work could start; the matter had to be sorted. It was
suggested that a rep from each trade approached the warring
parties with the aim of getting the main troublemakers off
the site. The contractor involved had agreed to keep his eyes
shut and give the committee a free hand. That afternoon a
group of six of us made our way to a piece of muddy ground,
in some places ankle-deep in water, where we found that the
troublemakers had set up a rough canvas awning as if to
announce that they were here to stay. There weren't more
than about a dozen of them which meant that actual physical
opposition would more than likely involve only three or four
of them.

The problem was what to do with the priest who, once we
had made our presence known, started waving his large, battered bible about and inciting his followers to see us off.
Seeing that I was the only Party member in the group I
thought that it was up to me to show some initiative. I faced
up to the bible-waving priest and told him in plain English
to 'shut 'is gob', language that all present understood, priest
or no priest. Then this big Irishman, who might have been
the leader of the pack, took a swipe at me which I dodged.
The lad had put so much effort into the swing that in missing me he lost his balance and slipped into the cold muddy
waters of a deep, evil smelling cesspool and under he went.
In a flash the mood of the lads round the pond changed as
everyone realised that the Paddy, who had not yet risen from
the murky depths, was in mortal danger. Two men jumped
in holding a rope and the luckless navvy was dragged to the
edge of the pond, covered from head to foot in slime and

excrement. A hose was produced from somewhere and in no time the lad and his rescuers were being washed down with freezing cold water. After that we didn't have any more trouble from them. In the months after, when the incident had passed into the history books, this part of the site was called 'The OK Corral'.

Having the leader down for the count might have proved the end for the intruders but not the end for little me. It was decided that facing down a priest was something that might remain a canker in our relationship with the Irish brothers. So there had to be a fall guy, who of course turned out to be yours truly.

The committee was very sorry, especially as I had taken the initiative in the incident, but an example had to be made. I was fined a week's pay which was to go into the site 'hard-up' fund. No sooner had this motion been carried than a second motion was proposed – a whip-round for Brother Gregg, all in favour, up went the hands, carried says the chairman. So all's well that ends well.

We all earned good money on these out-of-town sites but it was a way of earning a living that was completely different from the average building-site scene. You had to be able to handle yourself, not everyone's cup of tea you might say.

Leaving home at six or six thirty in the morning and not getting home until well past seven in the evening was taking its toll on our family relationships. It really shook me when, after a particularly hard day, I entered the flat at nearer eight than seven in the evening to be greeted by my nearly seven-year-old son: 'Hello, stranger.' To make matters worse I was beginning to get itchy feet again.

I gave it another week on the site, and the next Monday saw me up at Grafton Way, chatting up the union rep there

to set me up with a decent local employer. He got me a start
with a decorating firm up in Kentish Town; it was less than
half the wages I had been earning up at Borehamwood, but
the work was clean. Mr Brunsdon had connections with the
north London Catholic Church. Ninety per cent of his work
was the redecoration and upkeep of the schools and churches
in the area. He must have been on to a good thing because there
were never any calls about the job being in debt, the usual
spiel from any building employer. We took our time and
turned out some real first-class work. At twenty-nine I was
the youngest painter on the books. The best thing was that
the firm was 100 per cent union. When I showed Freda my
wage packet on the first week her only comment was, 'Well,
Vic, we carnt expect everything.' To me it seemed like being
in the depths of poverty.

I also had to explain to the union that I did not want to go
on doing Party work. Working for Brunsdon meant that my
life had slowed down, I had time to think and brood and less
than three weeks after my start I suffered a full night of terror. Freda woke me up, saying that I was shouting the house
down. I was wringing wet with sweat. In the morning Freda
suggested that I ought to see a doctor. 'It's years since you've
been like this, Vic, what's brought it all on?'

Freda took some time off from her little local job at the
dairy in Kenton Street to go up to Kentish Town and tell the
firm that I would be away for a few days. When she got back
home she told me, 'Mr Brunsdon is such a nice man and he
said that the foreman had said to him that Vic had been very
moody the last couple of days.' The foreman, who happened
to be ex-navy, had asked Freda about my war service. 'It
seems to be a nice firm you're working for now, Vic. Money
ain't everything and I'm hoping that this little bump I've

got is going to grow into a nice little girl and that things are going to get better.'

This was the first I had heard about Freda being pregnant.

'Why didn't you tell me when you first knew?'

'Because you've hardly ever been home long enough, all those hours you've been working, all this trade union stuff and then on a Sunday you're tearing up and down the roads of England trying to be the next champion of the world. It's about time you grew up, Vic, and started facing up to your responsibilities. We all love you but you're giving us a hard time. Think about it.'

On the whole my return to a normal life brought with it an improvement in our wife/husband relationship. Freda used to remark how lovely it was to have me home in the evening, and to tell the truth it did give me a happiness that had escaped me for the last six years. Sometimes Freda's mum came and sat with the kids while we went up west for a Saturday night out. Other times I took the kids up the local park to have a kick-about. Freda was over the moon. I was the normal husband and father at last, and to put the finishing touch on it I was at last working for a decent firm, earning reasonable money and coming home moderately clean.

Sometime about then news came round that Holborn Borough Council was poised to obey the instructions of the new Tory government and hand back the requisitioned houses they had turned into flats to accommodate the likes of Freda and our family. We decided to anticipate this by applying to the London County Council for a flat in the area. They offered us a small two-bedroom flat on the Bourne Estate just off the Gray's Inn Road. It was a bit pokey but we were a family again, and that was all that mattered.

Old man Brunsdon had a contract for a group of small offices in Clerkenwell Road. 'Just the job for you Gregg,' he says. I willingly agreed. Three minutes' walk around the corner and I'm on the job, couldn't be better. Then, one nice summer day, I walked home for a bit of dinner which Freda had on the table all ready.

'Where's Alan?'

'Oh, he's playing in the street with his friends.' Freda and I were sitting at the open window and I was enjoying the last few moments before setting off back to the job. 'Vic, I can hear our lad crying. What's going on?'

I poked my head out of the window and sure enough, right under our noses, there was a man holding our little boy by his collar and thumping him round the head. In the blink of an eye I'm out of the window and dropped the fifteen feet or so right on top of the bloke. At the same time I turned him and landed a couple of crisp right-handers. He went down like a stone. The man's wife was sitting in their car and saw everything. The woman was quick; she went straight to the police station just around the corner in the Gray's Inn Road. Three of the local lads pulled me off the man who was by now a bloody wreck and lying face down on the pavement. Freda had collected Alan and taken him up to the safety of the flat.

Later, two policemen arrived and carted me off to the nick where I was placed in a cell and informed that I would be charged the next morning with common assault.

My appearance at King's Cross Magistrates' Court the following day was short and sharp. My solicitor, a Mr Sedley, who later became a QC, said his piece about it being the God-given right for a man to protect his children. The beak replied that society needed protecting from ruffians like me.

'Fourteen days, take him down', whereupon Freda, who had insisted upon attending the proceedings, fainted.

I ended up doing seven days in Brixton, came out on appeal, but this was rejected so I had to go back and do the remaining seven days. On account of all this happening right on the doorstep of Fleet Street the national press had a field day. The magistrate, a Mr White, who had made a name for himself with other outlandish judgements, came in for a lot of stick. Didn't do me any good, though. I still had to do the time.

The warden in his uniform was quite an impressive character. His shiny silver buttons all seemed to be connected by various lengths of highly polished chain, one of which he was swinging backwards and forwards as if to balance himself against the huge array of big heavy keys he was carrying. He selected one and opened a heavy-looking green painted steel door, with a sliding vent which only opened from the outside. 'In you go, matey', and with a little pressure on my shoulder I'm propelled into this sanctuary, four bare walls painted a pale yellow with the lower part the same green as the door. One small grating with bars on the outside, that's the window, right up at ceiling level, a steel bed with a well-worn wire base and a mattress filled with some coir, two blankets and a pillow stuffed with the coir, same as the mattress. There was also a steel chair. The finishing touch was the toilet arrangements, two buckets, one of which was half filled with water which had an evil smelling disinfectant added to it.

The door slams shut and the sound of the warden's footsteps recedes. I sit on the bed; it's useless to try to look out of the window, it's too high up. The chair is uninviting; nothing to read, nothing to do. I spread the two blankets out, lay down on the bed and stare up at the ceiling. The vent in the door slides open. 'No lying on the beds until after five o'clock', then the vent slides shut. I begin to understand just how intimidating all this rigmarole can be to any normal citizen, but I quickly realise that I can cakewalk through this and it's going to serve as an experience. Ignoring the orders of the warden I stretched out on the bed and closed my eyes, waiting for the bell to clang out and signal the next meal. It wasn't the fourteen days that was the punishment, it was more of a rest from the daily slog. The real punishment was that with a criminal record I was barred from any job that involved dealing with the general public.

Even tucked away inside one of her Majesty's hotels I managed to blot my copybook. I was detailed to join a gang of the inmates and we were marched to a long corrugated-iron shed and instructed in the art of sewing mailbags. 'Remember, it's eight stitches to the inch.' To make sure we stuck to regulation stitching we were each handed a strip of brass that had lines stamped on its surface, just like a ruler. I stick this routine for about thirty minutes and up goes my hand. 'You go to the toilet in the break,' shouts the warden from his seat, which is a couple of feet higher than the prisoners' level. 'I don't want the toilet, Mister, I want to know, before I do another stitch, the rate for the job!'

Silence reigned, but only for a few moments, and then the shed erupted, hands clapping, much clomping of heavy boots along with the usual catcalls. The warden wasted no time. He pressed the button by his seat and almost immediately a squad of wardens descended on the shed. I'm lifted off my feet by a couple of them and the next thing is that I'm standing in front of the prison guv'nor, who reads me what I suppose is the riot act. I'm told to knuckle down and accept the punishment. 'If you come up in front of me again you'll be in here for twenty-eight days.' With that I'm marched down to my cell. To be fair, the guv'nor did say that he thought the punishment handed out to me was a bit on the harsh side considering the circumstances. His parting shot was: 'My advice to you is do your time and make the best of it.' Then I was marched back to my cell.

When I had served my sentence I returned to Brunsdon's to thank the boss for paying my wages for the fortnight I had been away. Freda was in the money because not only did Brunsdon's pay my wages, but the union branch also stepped in with a sizable donation.

Another time there was a big London rally against German rearmament when thousands of angry protesters turned up. The next morning it was Freda's turn to parade in front of the magistrates, along with a dozen or so other women. They were charged with disturbing the peace. They'd gone into the Visitors' gallery at the House of Commons and when the subject of rearmament was brought up they showered the MPs below with leaflets. They were locked up in the cells of the House of Commons and the next morning were brought before the beak, who bound them over to keep the peace. The group I was with were all fined twenty quid each for carrying offensive weapons.

Another spot of bother came over the execution in America of the husband and wife pair Ethel and Julius Rosenberg. This cruel event took place in June 1953. The Rosenbergs had been accused of spying for the Soviets and there was little doubt that they were guilty, but to fry the two of them in the electric chair was inhuman. On the night President Eisenhower signed the death warrant the whole of the West End was brought to a standstill; the police were powerless.

There were thousands of people stretching from Oxford Street to Trafalgar Square. There were similar scenes in all the capital cities of Europe; even the Pope put in his twopenn'orth. The fifties and the sixties were a time when a lot of people got involved with politics. I imagine that Freda and I, belonging as we did to the most influential Communist Party branch in central London, had our cards well and truly marked by the powers that be in national security.

6

On the Road

By now, Freda had given birth to our third child, a little girl who we christened Judith. Old man Brunsdon was due to take a holiday but before he went he took on a job in Chapel Street up near Marble Arch. This meant lugging a handcart from Kentish Town, loaded up with all the gear – steps, ladders, scaffold boards, about six heavy dustsheets and all the rest of the odd bits and pieces that are needed on a decent sized decorating job. Terry, the lad I normally worked with, refused to take the job on. Terry was ex-navy and as stubborn as an ox. I didn't want the job either but to please the old man I volunteered to give it a go as long as he gave me a couple of labourers to push the cart and someone to replace Terry, someone who could keep up with my pace of work. On the following Monday I'm up in Chapel Street, the cart turns up at midday, pushed by two big sweating labourers and Terry's replacement, a chap I'd never set eyes on before. He didn't look much to me. I asked him if he had a card. 'No, I don't believe in trade unions.' I told him, no card, no job, take it or leave it. I'm certain the lad (like the rest of the men on the firm) had no taste for the daily journey to this out-of-the-way job, so with the help of the two labourers I finally get the cart unloaded and get ready to start the next day.

The next morning I'm on the job bright and early. I make a start on the suite of offices on the top floor. By midday I'm halfway through the initial preparation, but back in Kentish Town old man Brunsdon's son was undoing all of his dad's good work. The boy had taken over the running of the business while his father was away. When he learned that I had sent the other painter back to base because he didn't have a union card, he did his nut.

The result was that while I was sitting down eating the sandwiches that Freda had packed for me I heard footsteps on the stairs and muffled swearing and cursing. In burst the yard foreman, and he was doing his nut as well. After standing there effing and blinding he cools down enough to explain the displeasure I had caused by sending the new painter back.

'He'll be back tomorrow and Mr John is docking your wages for the day.'

'Is he now! I'll tell you what, Tom, you go back to the yard and get the girl to make up my cards. I'll be along tomorrow to collect them.'

'Don't be stupid, Vic, the old man will sort it all out when he gets back, you know that.'

'Maybe, Tom, maybe not, nobody threatens me. Didn't Terry warn the silly sod how I would take it?'

'Terry don't know anything about it yet. I'm worried now that he might take the same attitude as you.'

'Don't worry about Terry,' I said, 'he's been with the old man since he was demobbed, he feels he's part of the firm, he'll 'ave words with the guv'nor and the old man will chew the balls off our Mr John. I'll be along in the morning to return the keys.' And with that I started packing up my tools, tied them on the back of my bike and was away.

Looking back I should have stayed with Brunsdon; he was a good employer, a man who really looked after the lads who worked for him.

I came home that afternoon to an empty flat. Freda was still at her job in the dairy. They've all disappeared now but in those days they were thriving small businesses, generally run by a husband and wife. The man usually got up well before the crack of dawn delivering the milk to his customers' doorsteps while the wife held the fort in the shop. Freda's dairy was owned by a couple we met when we were living in Kenton Street. The husband was Welsh and during his last couple of months in the army he had been stationed in Belgium where he had met this strapping young Belgian girl. He brought her back to England, married her and with the help of his mum and dad back in Cardiff started up a dairy. Freda was friendly with the pair of them and she offered to help them out for about five hours a day. Freda looked after the shop from midday while the couple got their heads down for a couple of hours of well-earned shut-eye. One of the more famous customers was Tommy Cooper, the popular British comedian.

When she got home Freda was surprised to see me. 'You're back early, Vic.' Then I told her the whole sorry tale. 'Have the rest of the week off, Vic, you deserve it. You've been slogging your guts out for the last couple of years.'

'No way, love, you know that I could never stand the idleness of just hanging around. I'll have a nose round tomorrow, I'll soon get another job, no trouble, easy as falling off a log.' We both set out to collect our younger boy from his nursery school. The older lad could look after himself until we got back.

The next day sees me up at Penton Street, the Labour
Exchange. I had decided to give the union offices a miss. I had
no desire to get involved with any more union or Party work,
I'd had a gutful. I wanted to get a job, earn some money and
enjoy the wife and kids. But the Labour Exchange only came
up with a couple of starts that weren't worth looking at, so I
made my way over to the pub opposite the Exchange and I'm
about to put the cash on the bar to pay for the drink when a
hand reaches in front of me and slaps down a ten bob note.

I turned around to face my benefactor. It took me about
fifteen seconds before I recognised the chap, another Terry,
but a very different breed from the one I had just parted
company with.

We sat down and started with the usual questions and
answers.

Under normal circumstances I would probably have given
this ghost from my past a very wide birth. This Terry had a
reputation for being a very hard man. The last time we had
been together was when we shared one of Dickie Bird's carriers way back in '41 at Sidi Rezegh in North Africa. Terry's
driver had taken a piece of shrapnel between the eyes and I
had been ordered to take his place. We soldiered together for
the next three or four months and had learned in a very hard
school to trust each other when the chips were not just down
but at rock bottom.

'Ain't yer working, Vic?'

'On and off, Terry, more off than on.'

'I can fix you up with a good earner if you're prepared to
graft.'

This pub in Penton Street was one of my favourites. Freda's
dad had introduced me to it when I had come home from
Italy way back in 1943. Part of the attraction was that no

hard drinks were sold. It was what in those days was called a beer house. The clientele consisted of men who only wanted a nice quiet place to have a natter and enjoy a swig of Colonel Whitbread's best. It was a good place to relax after being booted out of the Labour Exchange across the road. 'Never been in 'ere before, Vic, not bad is it?' Terry gives the publican the thumbs-up, and after a short natter about the ins and outs of the job he's telling me about we saunter off down Pentonville Hill and end up on a large tract of waste ground behind the gasworks at the back of King's Cross Station. It was a cleaned-up bombsite and had been leased out to the present tenants by the Gas Light and Coke Company. The area was enclosed by a six-foot-high galvanised corrugated-iron fence.

Terry led me up to a medium-size shed, built with the same galvanised sheeting as the surrounding wall, banged on the door and introduced me to a couple of bruisers who were lounging in two battered armchairs. One had a fag in his mouth, the other, a much larger individual, was smoking the remains of a cigar that smelt like something dragged out of a farmyard. Terry led off.

'This is Vic, an old mate of mine. 'e's interested in the job.'

The more junior looking of the two sitting in the arm-chairs eyed Terry. 'Is 'e kosher then?' Well, the pair of them didn't look Jewish to me so perhaps that was just their way of talking.

'Vic's OK, he can 'andle 'imself.'

'Down to you then, Terry. Anyfing goes wrong you're in for a going over.' This threat didn't seem to bother Terry one bit.

'Come with me, Vic, I'll show yer the motor you'll be driving, it's already loaded, two drops in Manchester, a real doddle.' Instead of telling me about the job Terry suggests that we go over to the local café and 'ave a cuppa and a natter, which we do.

'You're the first I've met of the old lot, Vic. I did go to one of the dinners down in Bow Road but I didn't meet anyone I knew, ain't been interested since. What about yourself, you married?' Terry was hungry for news of the old days when we were surrounded by men we could trust and have a laugh and joke with.

It was only an hour and a half since Terry had slapped down that ten shilling note in front of me up in the Whitbread's pub and in that time his whole demeanour had changed. From being a man fully in control he had changed into someone haunted by a ghost. I recognised the signs. Changing the subject, I mentioned to Terry that I had bumped into Georgie Foulks about a month ago. Terry's eyes lit up again.

'Georgie boy! What you don't know, Vic, is that me and Georgie signed on the same day, it was at the barracks up in Harrow Road. Nineteen thirty-five it was. 'Ow is he then?'

I told Terry that his old mate had just been released from one her Majesty's hotels and that I didn't think it would be too long before he was inside again.

'Georgie may 'ave been a right crook but 'e was a right good mate to 'ave if you were in a tight corner.' To which I readily agreed. 'You'll meet blokes just like George on this job, Vic, we've got a couple working for us right now, right dodgy customers they may be, but not to their mates. Come on, Vic, I'll show you around.' With that we strolled off to the piece of waste ground at present tenanted by the pair who I would come to know as the infamous Dawson brothers.

Terry took me round the back of a larger shed and there it was resting on its eight wheels, loaded, roped and sheeted, ready to go. 'Blimey, Terry, we had these old beasts in the desert in 'forty-one. Is it a runner?'

'No problem, Vic. Andy and 'is bruvver bought eight of them in a government auction, all brand new. All they had to do was to put another cab on the front, they'll run them till they collapse and then get some new gear. There's one problem with them. They still have that old army gearbox; with the best will in the world it's thirty-five top whack unless of course you're going downhill out of cog, in which case the brakes are dodgy. And one more thing, Vic, forget about shagging the wife every night, you'll have to save it all for Saturday.' Terry gives me a grin as if to say, 'Sorry, mate, that's the way it is.' Then he said, 'The plus side to all of this is that while the rest of the potty workers are existing on twenty or so a week you'll be clearing a ton at the very least – the job's yours if you can do it, Vic.'

Terry, having started chatting, didn't seem to want to stop. 'You'll be in good company here, Vic, they've all bin through the mill, all in the same boat as us, all of them properly fucked up in mind and thought. These people who 'ave been civvies all of their life will never understand the likes of us, not as long as they 'ave a hole in their arse. I bet my bottom dollar it's the same wiv you. All of us will always be square pegs trying to fit into round 'oles.

'You remember 'ow we used to talk about our girlfriends back in Blighty? Well, I married Daisy, she put up wiv me for a whole year then she ups and does a flit. Never seen or heard from her since. I've got an arrangement wiv one of the

girls I used to go to school wiv, she's a pro, working out of
Lisle Street, she comes around to my patch every month or
so, we spend a week together then she's off and we're back
on our lonesome until we feel like a bit of company again. It
works out OK for both of us.' Terry points to a smallish chap
who's roping up one of the big eight-wheelers. 'That's Ted
Vincent, we all call him Vinnie, he's an ex-rear gunner, RAF
Bomber Command, lasted out the whole scene since nineteen
forty-one. He survived right through, don't ever rub 'im
up the wrong way, Vic, 'e carries a knife in that back pocket.
'is brain is gorn, Vic, but as long as 'e does the job for the
brothers he will never be short of graft, 'e's a decent bloke
when he's normal.' Terry carried on as if he never wished to
stop. 'None of us lads 'ere will ever fit in if yer ask me, Vic,
we're all fucked up.'

And that was my introduction, via Terry, to the murky
and mainly lawless world of long-distance road haulage, an
industry that existed by breaking every law in the book. In
doing so it kept Britain's trade lifelines from the factories to
the docks going full steam ahead.

I go home to tell the wife that I'm about to earn a fortune
but don't expect me home each week until Saturday. Freda,
who had heard the bit about earning a fortune many times
in the past two years, gave a grimace. 'I don't like the idea of
you being away from us like that. We've been settling down
nicely these last couple of months. What you're telling me
now is that we will only see you at weekends. It makes me
think you're glad to see the back of us! Money ain't everything, Vic.'

'Not to worry, Freda, I'll do the job for a couple of months,
get some cash in the bank and then give it the drop kick.'
She gave me a look as if to say, 'I've heard all that before.'

As Terry had said, the two brothers had acquired these army surplus motors at a government auction. A couple had been written off in the first month due to the drivers employed not having either the strength or the experience to keep the beasts on the road and in a straight line. One of the lads had been killed outright, the other was still getting straightened out at Highgate General Hospital up Archway Hill.

There wasn't much chance of falling asleep at the wheel of these massive ex-army eight-wheelers. The suspension was noticeable by its absence, and, of course, in those days power steering was a dream of the gods; the battle was constant and the winner had to be the driver, or else!

As the weeks progressed I got to know the rest of the lads. Almost to a man they were ex-service, men who were uncomfortable taking orders, all of them quite capable of starting and finishing a war on their own. At least half of them were in the same boat as myself, married with kids and unable to cope with the responsibilities of marriage. Their solution was to earn as much as they could to keep the wife and kids well fed and clothed. They all claimed to love their families and yet they anchored themselves to a form of employment that was as dangerous as it was anti-social.

The brothers had a contract with a timber importer from Silvertown. When a shipment arrived at the Surrey Docks the wagons went down and loaded up from what turned out to be Russian ships. A lot of timber that was being used in the United Kingdom was coming through those docks from Russia.

The long shed in the corner of the site at King's Cross was used as a storage shed for the wood. The importer sent the brothers a delivery note with addresses all over the country.

The advantage was that the importer didn't have to pay extra storage costs if the trade slowed down, plus the brothers could do a bit of timber dealing on the side without having to buy the product – 500 square feet of timber would never be missed from the continual loads coming in from the Surrey Docks. The Dawsons also owned a large warehouse at Stoke-on-Trent which they shared with a family of crooks who ran a transport firm operating out of a bombsite in the centre of Birmingham. It was about three months before I was let into the bonus work of transporting loads to Stoke. The loads were all bent and as a result fifty quid was added to the weekly pay packet. I was getting paid sums that the unions could only dream about.

As if the profits from all of this illegal trafficking weren't enough the brothers had a spare driver, 'Phil the boxer', whose vehicle was a huge furniture van. The brothers used to get a phone call and off went this pot-bellied old pugilist to some transport café stuck up on one of Britain's trunk roads. He got his nickname 'Phil' because of Phil Scot, a former British heavyweight boxing champion who spent so much time on the floor of the ring that he was called 'The Horizontal Champion'. Phil would arrive at the café at a given time, transfer a load of whatever and then take it down to Silvertown where the brothers rented another warehouse right on the banks of the river – all very mysterious and illegal. The Dawson brothers got away with their criminal activities because the whole of the British road transport system was in on the fiddle. The drivers, the loaders, the stevedores at the docks and the clerks who filled in non-existent returns. All of them had their fingers in the pie.

My time with the brothers Dawson and their collection of army-reject eight-wheelers lasted for the next nine or so months but came to a sudden halt when the police raided the firm's warehouse in Silvertown and took possession of thousands of pounds' worth of stolen goods, mainly cigarettes and whisky, radios and the like. Phil the Boxer was the only driver on the firm to go down with the brothers; as far as the rest of us were concerned we were all legit. The police padlocked the site and we were on the stones again, but while it lasted we all earned a fortune.

With the demise of the Dawson brothers' operation I was forced to report back to the branch at King's Cross and offer my humble apologies, telling them why I had been away for the last nine months. I knew they would find me something that earned a decent wage; after all, we were all comrades, all in the struggle for the working classes. 'Get up to Borehamwood, Vic, there's a lot of work up there.' In no time at all there I was selling the *Daily Worker* at the gates of the site and doing my part to ensure that only card holders got the jobs. I stuck it for almost a year.

I learned every trick in the book about keeping men organised. It was a huge development and there were construction and civil engineering firms involved. The Party had a branch on site and we were the only people who took the trade union movement to heart. We tried our hardest to get all the lads to attend site meetings and so it was the Party who kept the sites in order. When some trade had a grudge against the firm they were working for it was to the Party branch on site they almost always turned. We always arranged a meeting with the firm's reps and without too much trouble the differences were usually sorted. The firm's overbearing foreman, or whoever had caused the upset, would be removed and sent somewhere else. The last thing anybody wanted, especially the employers, was a stoppage. Those sites were very tough places to work and what the Party had was discipline. We met twice a week and talked about the problems. All in all there were only about ten thousand Party members in the country but, in my opinion, we were as strong as the British Army at the height of the Empire.

My job was to attend the regular meetings and represent the King's Cross Branch. I readily admit I enjoyed crossing swords with anyone in power. It suited my hatred of unchecked authority, but all this took time and the drawback was that the real life that I should have been enjoying, the building of a family life, respect from the kids and love from Freda was once again at risk of being thrown down the pan.

Eventually Freda cracked and we had a right royal bust-up. It happened because I had to spend a couple of days in hospital because of a punch-up over a disagreement. The violence that burnt inside me was never far from the surface. Freda decided that it was time to read the riot act and make me see the error of my ways, but she was bashing her head against a brick wall. Things were getting bad and I couldn't see the warning signs. Terry, the chap who had introduced me to the Dawsons, took me to task one Saturday morning in the local pub in Somers Town. We were waiting for the guv'nor to come up with the wages. Terry suddenly said, 'What's with these moods you keep getting, Vic? You keep stirring the shit here and you're going to end up with a right thumping.' I said, 'Nobody orders me around, understand, Terry, I take it from nobody.' 'Just giving you the word, Vic, we all get the shakes now and again, you ain't the only one that's been through the shit.' Terry meant well but his words bounced off me like a ball against a brick wall.

The word came to one of our meetings that a good Party man was needed to chair the union branch of a big haulage firm in Stratford, east London. I was bored with the building industry and, more to the point, the daily trek up to Borehamwood. I put my name forward and in a couple of weeks I was duly installed. The firm was so large that controlling the workforce was left to the union branch. This was not unusual, because the bonus systems meant that the employees toed the line and kept their noses to the grindstone, and as long as production carried on unhindered the management was satisfied.

One Saturday morning I was sitting in our local café, waiting for the midday whistle before disappearing for the weekend when one of the lads came in saying there was a carload of the filth parked outside and they were asking questions about the whereabouts of a Mr Gregg. At that point all the lads did a quick scarper. I went outside to investigate.

Once they knew that I was the one they were looking for, everything became very friendly.

'We're only here for a chat, Mr Gregg. We understand that you and your mates are up before the local beak, disturbing the peace, is that it?'

'You've got it right – you're not the law are you?'

'Tell us, Vic, what's a bloke with a war record like you doing playing around with a bunch of Commies? Your last employer, we are given to understand, is doing three years.

We're here to offer you a chance of a nice clean job where you will come home every night, clean and tidy and more or less set your own terms.'

Then they told me that the court appearance had been fixed, and we were all off the hook.

'No need to look surprised, Mr Gregg, your army records and files are an open book as far we are concerned. We know all about you and the Party and we know that quite soon you are going to be visited by one of your Party officials in the road transport office. He's going to ask you to take a job as a chauffeur to the chairman of Moscow Bank, just around the corner from where you live, Finsbury Circus to be exact. It's in our interests that you take the job, but in all fairness and to be blunt, whether you take the job or not is none of our business, but you must be aware that if you carry on in the manner in which you've carried on since you were demobbed, sooner or later you're going to end up in the nick. Have a think about it. We're not asking you to inform on your mates, just those foreign Commie bastards at the bank. Considering the time you spent with Popski, this should be right up your street. See you around, Victor.' Then the man who had being doing all this chat opened the car door, got in, gave me a short wave and was off.

I was shaken by the reference to Popski, or Major Vladimir Peniakoff, to give him his full title. I was seconded to Popski in early 1941 after some very heavy fighting in North Africa. I used to carry messages and stuff around for him and if the enemy had got their hands on me I would have been shot on the spot. I wondered what they wanted to do now, whoever 'they' were.

It was a Saturday morning and I made my way back to the yard where the lads were loading and sheeting up the wagon for me to drive to Manchester first thing Monday morning. It was pay day but instead of going down the pub with the others I hopped on my little Francis-Barnet two-stroke and went home.

After ruminating for a long time and wondering how these people knew so much about me, I decided that if the offer they talked about came I would accept it. It would make the kids and Freda happy if I had a regular job where I was home every night.

I decided to keep mum and said nothing to Freda. As it turned out I only had to wait a couple of weeks. It came at the end of a particularly heavy week's work. I had done two Manchester loads and a long West Country load of reinforced steel. I was well and truly knackered. The kids were sitting in the corner on the floor playing cards, Freda was ploughing through a Jane Austen novel, and as far as I can remember I was probably fast akip after the evening meal. Then we get a knock on the door. There he was, Tom Harding, the Party's area rep. Freda gave him her usual friendly greeting.

'Hello, Tom, haven't seen you about for a few weeks!'

'I've been sent round to have a chat with Vic. I've come to ask if he would be willing to drop his present vocation of charging around Britain and getting nowhere and take on a nice well-paid job where he will be home every night as clean and well pressed as he was when he left for work in the morning.' Tom Harding didn't hold the job of area rep by being stupid. He knew that by saying 'home every night' and the bit about being 'clean and well pressed' he had the wife on his side. I agreed to attend an interview.

For the next couple of weeks I carried on slogging my way
backwards and forwards along the highways and byways of
Britain, using any lay-by I could find to catch a few hours'
kip in the cab. The life of the long-distance lorry driver was
a twenty-four-hour-a-day job, the reward being the weekly
pay packet, which was far more than anything I could earn
in an office or factory. It was also a life fraught with danger.
It was all too easy to be lulled off to sleep by the monoto-
nous throb of a big diesel engine and the hum of the tyres
on the tarmacked road surface. The journey was often inter-
rupted by the flashing lights of police cars and ambulances,
the wrecks of overloaded eight-wheelers, most probably
lying in a ditch with the drivers dead. The law said that
eleven hours was the maximum amount of time you could
drive. The only firms and their drivers who obeyed these
laws were the government-owned transport firms.

For us the daylight hours were used to unload, then off
to the nearest clearing house to pick up a fresh load. In
London it was usually one of the huge docks. The motor-
ways did not exist at that time and the three main arteries
were the A4 to the west; the A1, or Great North Road, was
the main route to Scotland and the north, while the busi-
est and most dangerous of the lot was the A5, considered
to be the lifeline of British industry. During the daylight
hours this was a normal main road but around 8 or 9 p.m.
it was a different matter when the first of the night's lorry
drivers eased their overloaded eight-wheelers and artics
up the incline of Barnet Hill and through the gateways
of St Albans and Hatfield, prepared to drive until early
morning. These roads carried an endless stream of heavy
vehicles, all of them pumping huge black clouds of diesel
fumes into the houses of the luckless citizens who lived in

the towns and villages along the way. This was the life I was being asked to put aside, and for what? Being a paid lackey to some fat slob of a bank chairman? Somebody had got to be joking.

7

The Ace of Spades

The interview with the bank chairman was scheduled for the following Wednesday, the day when the firm collected a weekly load of carbon black from the docks for delivery to the Firestone Tyre factory on the Great West Road. The firm kept a spare trailer for this particular job as it was almost impossible to clean it for any other sort of delivery. The work was so dirty that we took turns to do it, encouraged by a substantial bonus, paid by Firestone's themselves. So, Sod's Law, Wednesday was my turn.

On Tuesday night Freda spent an hour sponging and pressing my only suit, the usual one, the one I had been demobbed in, placing it in a freshly cleaned and ironed pillowcase. She instructed me to 'make sure you change out of them filthy clothes before you go in to the interview'.

In the morning I reported to the loading bay at the East India Docks, ready for the crane to start loading a cargo that coated everything within three hundred yards with thick, black, sticky dust. When the dust settled, which took an hour, I set off for Firestone's. Me being me, there was no way I was going all the way to Chiswick, back to the docks and then on to Finsbury Circus. No, I was going to fit the interview in en route.

About two in the afternoon my filthy Atkinson unit, dragging a forty-foot trailer loaded with the infamous carbon black, anchored up outside the premises of the Moscow Bank at Finsbury Circus. No sooner had the vehicle shuddered to a halt when clouds of carbon began to descend on to the glistening Rolls-Royces and Daimlers parked up waiting for the City's elite. The unit's battery was knackered which meant I had to leave the engine running, so the area was filled with the fumes of diesel which swirled in a thick black cloud over this hub of London's financial world.

I had not even jumped out of the cab before things began to go wrong. I found myself in front of a small, officious gentleman wearing a big brass badge on a chain around his neck. He told me that he was in charge of the goings on around the Circus and that I must 'remove this vehicle at once'. I didn't take the slightest bit of notice. Soon all the chauffeurs were swearing and cursing about the state of their cars, the prized Rollers and Daimlers. There were clouds of black soot and diesel fumes everywhere – I might as well have been a chimney sweep.

I opened the main door of the bank and was hit by the noise of a busy office, something very strange to me. The clatter of typewriters, the chatter of conversation and the sight of people walking from desk to desk. I had arrived in a new world.

Once people saw me, the noise slowly died down. Up came a beady eyed individual who demanded to know what I was doing there. So I explained my position, that I had an appointment with the chairman of the bank, saying at the same time, 'I don't know his name. Just tell him that I'm from King Street.' The beady eyed individual was the bank's secretary and he escorted me through the main office into a large room that was dominated by a long mahogany table that seemed to stretch the whole length of the room, and a couple of large portraits that adorned two of the otherwise bare walls. The largest and most important of the two portraits was of a genial smiling ruffian of a man with a large pipe stuck between his lips. This was Stalin, painted so that whatever part of the room you were in, it seemed that the eyes of the 'great man' were fixed on you. The other, smaller portrait, was of Lenin, standing on a rostrum and waving his arms in the air as if pleading with the comrades to go forward into battle.

There were three men sitting at the table. In prime position was a bald-headed individual, unsmiling, sporting a three-day beard, his shirt undone at the neck and minus a collar and tie. Much to my surprise, and disappointment, this scruff was the number one man who asked me through his interpreter, 'Could Mr Gregg make a start next Monday?' The 'scruff' was the chairman of the bank, who was totally unfazed by my appearance. I had contrived to look as filthy as possible to ensure that I would be rejected there and then. This man, whose name, I found out, was Alexie Chernuzube, was definitely the top dog, not much doubt about that. Nobody around the table queried his decision. I must have been the filthiest individual ever to darken the portals of the Moscow Narodny Bank, but Chernuzube had sized me up and made his decision without a moment's hesitation.

Next day, when I reported to the garage and said I wanted my cards the yard manager did his top. I had the distinct impression that he wanted to discuss my request for my cards in the alley at the back of the garage. To be fair, I had given him little notice and it wasn't easy to find the type of men willing to put up with the chaotic conditions of long-distance lorry driving. In the end we shook hands and parted.

When I reported to the bank the following Monday I was told by the manager that the job had been taken:

'Some scruffy sod came in last Wednesday and got the job.'

'Yep, that's me, mate, I'm the scruffy sod, and before I start work I would like to go into the question of wages.'

'Nothing to discuss. You can start at the same wages as the chauffeur you're replacing.' Then the gimlet-eyed, portly manager retreated into his office.

He seemed surprised when he opened his door to my knock.

'Yes, Mr Gregg?'

'I asked about the wages, you haven't replied.'

'Come in and sit down and you can sign a couple of papers that we will need.'

I was quite cool up to this point. 'I noticed the name on the door. Mr Turner. Is that you?'

'Yes, indeed that's me and I am general secretary to the chairman of the bank. If you ever have a complaint or query I'm the person you come to.'

'Well, Mr Turner, my name is Mr Gregg and I have been asked to take on this job and I tell you right now, it's against my better judgement.' I paused to let what I had said sink in. 'Now, I will ask once more, how much is this job worth?'

The gentleman sitting on the other side of the table seemed to be at a loss as to how to answer my simple request. 'It's simple enough, Mr Turner, how much do I get paid?'

'Mr Gregg, the bank has decided to be very generous in your case. It is usual to pay a newcomer of your ranking thirty-five pounds a month, but we have decided to give you the full forty pounds a month of twenty-eight days; you also get luncheon vouchers for five days a week and we will supply you with appropriate clothing for the job. After the first six months you will be eligible for the bank's pension scheme.' There he stopped and shut the drawer of his desk as if to terminate the interview.

'In that case, Mr Turner, you had better go and inform your chairman that he still needs a chauffeur.' It was obvious to me that this Mr Turner had never had to face up to an underling questioning the decisions of the bank. I decided to offer him some assistance.

'I'll tell you what, Mr Turner, it's eleven o'clock now. I'm going to disappear for a couple of hours; I'll be back at two this afternoon. Let's start talking at eighty a month and I will throw in the first five hours of any overtime at the normal rate, that's eighty divided by forty.'

I left the building and walked off to find a pub where I could get a cheese roll and a pint of Charrington's best. I was feeling good. I was not going to buckle under to anyone in authority, whatever their political convictions. I was certain that Freda would never let me work for £10 a week, not after I had been handing over a minimum of fifty or so every week. It never occurred to me that I was being unreasonable; after all, I was being offered the standard for lower ranking staff in any of the big five banks.

I went back that afternoon congratulating myself on having found an easy way to refuse the job. Turner greeted me and he led me to the large room where I had been interviewed. The chairman, speaking through his interpreter, asked me why I had asked for such a large sum of money. I explained that I didn't reckon that £80 a month was a lot. Chernuzube thanked me and said the bank would pay me £70 a month. I agreed on condition that I was included in any percentage wage increase given to the rest of the bank staff. This appeared to satisfy Chernuzube, but Turner had a face like thunder. I learned soon after I started the job that the two top English members of staff, the secretary and the accountant, only drew a wage of ninety a month, and they had spent years on the job.

The work started off in a tame enough way. After dropping the chairman off at his house in West Hill, I garaged the car in the lock-up in Highgate Village, jumped aboard my little Francis-Barnet 125 motorcycle and I was home and dry by six at the latest. After three days I was bored stiff. I felt as if I was sleepwalking through life, although on the plus side Freda was happy and our life together began to regain the love and happiness that bit by bit we had been losing. This was why I disciplined myself to stay with it and give the job time.

I knew why I had been shanghaied into this chauffering work, although at first all that happened was the occasional appearance by a couple of men, always the same, asking me how things were going and telling me to keep my ears and eyes open. They always turned up on the same day and at the same time every week. 'Getting bored with the job already, mate? Looks to us that you've landed a real cushy number, just jot it down if you have to pick up anyone out of the ordinary.' Then they strolled off, as if they were just a couple of tourists asking for directions.

The boredom did not last. The bank was not a normal bank and sometimes the hours got very erratic, depending on what was happening in the world and even more, inside the walls of the Kremlin. Meetings could go on far into the night and I was expected to be on call all the time. This had an impact on life at home and after a while Freda began to have her doubts about the new life I was leading.

One night, after a fortnight of working late, I came home to find Freda sitting on our old two-seater settee with her knees tucked under her chin and tears streaming down her face. I knelt down to be level with her and tried to put my arms around her, but she pushed me away. I couldn't get through to her, all my protestations fell on deaf ears. Then, without warning, she looked me straight in the eye and began to talk.

'I don't know why you bother to come home at all. I think you are using this job as an excuse to keep away from us. Why don't you just up and leave? It's obvious any love you might have had for me and the kids is long gone.' She kept on and on like this until I finally went into our little kitchen and made a cup of tea which Freda accepted, and then she went off to bed. When I finally joined her I found that she had made no effort to get undressed.

I fell asleep and some time later was woken up by Freda shaking me. She was standing over me, still dressed, holding a towel and a bowl of water. The bed clothes were scattered all over the place and I was sweating like a pig. Freda began to bathe my face and said she was sorry for the way she had behaved and I was to forget all that stuff she had said about me not loving her. Then she said, 'But you've got to see a doctor, Vic, you've been raving like a maniac for the last couple of hours – you've probably woken up the whole building. I don't know what gets into you, you never used to be like this. I think you should pack this job in Vic. If you get some proper sleep every night we'll get ourselves sorted, I know we will.'

I have thought about this incident a lot over the years and wondered what sort of demon was living inside me that made me so difficult to live with, that drove me to be constantly doing things, never at peace, always looking for excitement and distraction. It was like I was when I was riding on the bike, lost in a physical world that stopped me from thinking about all the stuff I had seen in the war. Freda thought that all I had to do was get an easy job, earn enough to keep us all off the breadline and we'd all be in clover. If only!

8

Serving Two Masters

It was the middle of November 1953 and I was standing in a doorway on the corner of Regent Street and Marlborough Street. There was an arctic wind blowing over the whole of southern Britain and I'm thinking that there has to be a better way to earn a crust than what I'm doing now.

I've got my eyes peeled on the impressive portico of the Dynasty restaurant, regarded by those who know as the best Chinese restaurant in London. The Chinese Embassy have decided in their wisdom to introduce one of their visiting dignitaries to the capital, and they are doing it in style. Normally they held these affairs in the secrecy of their embassy in Portland Place.

My quarry was an obscure official in the Romanian Embassy who my masters, the Russians, have reason to believe is earning a bit on the side by giving away Russian trade secrets. I'm being paid on this freezing night to find out if this is true. The Romanian Embassy have planted stuff on him which he thinks is the real hot stuff; naturally it's all a big con but our man is unaware of this. So there I am, freezing my balls off and waiting to see if this man leaves the restaurant on his own, and, if he does, try to find out who he meets up with or if he is meeting people he shouldn't – like the Americans.

I can see him saying goodnight to his cronies and then walking off in the direction of Oxford Street as if he was going to catch a bus to his flat near the Romanian Embassy. At that moment the rain started coming down in torrents. The tall figure I was following was wrapped up nice and warm under an umbrella. I, on the other hand, was getting wetter by the minute.

It was now well past ten and I was about to give the whole scheme the drop kick when the man disappeared into the small Lyons restaurant on the eastern side of the Underground station at Oxford Circus. I managed to grab a stool next to the steamed-up window near the door and settled in to await developments. Then two men approached my quarry and were so obviously American that I decided I had achieved my purpose for the night. Soon I was aboard a bus and in twenty minutes I was opening the door to our small council flat in Portpool Lane. Shortly after that I was explaining to the wife that I'd had a hell of a night. Freda looked at my dripping wet figure and knew I was not up to any infidelities.

'Come on, Vic, we'll 'ave a nice cup of tea and snuggle up in bed.' One thing was certain: there was to be no turning up at the bank at nine the next morning. If they wanted me to do these kinds of tricks then I was going to work what hours I saw fit.

A sudden change in my work happened when a new member of the bank, a Russian, Georg Borovitch, turned up via the branch in Washington DC. I never knew what his official role was. He was the odd man out and never seemed to have a regular job like the rest of the staff.

To compete in the global world of commerce the Russians needed information, and they tried to get it by any means, fair or foul. Industrial espionage was the name of the new game, and as I was to learn over the next few years Georgie was an expert at it.

He was a tall, handsome man, with a nice manner. He spoke quietly and politely with a slight American twang. He had the look of someone who was open and honest and was able to charm his way wherever he went. It seemed to me that Georgie boy was a top-level industrial spy.

After he had graced the bank with his presence for about three months or so, Georgie started to commandeer more of my time. One day he appeared in my small rest room, his face wreathed in a huge smile, rubbing his hands together. 'Get your coat on, Victor, we're going out.' That was the start of it. Our first destination was usually the trade delegation house on West Hill, north of Kentish Town, and from there to anywhere which was usually any one of a number of West End hotels or restaurants in or around Marble Arch, Piccadilly and the like. Sometimes it was a private address, but that was rare. In the car Georgie kept up a never-ending stream of light-hearted chatter. I think he was checking me out and in the end must have been satisfied that he had me well and truly sussed.

So we settled into a routine. What used to happen was that before we set off on a round of visits I was sent to the National Provincial Bank with one of the bank messengers, and there we would fill a suitcase with money. Soon after that, within a couple of days I would be detailed to cart Georgie on one of his round trips. I wasn't exactly the bagman so much as the bagman's driver. We would arrive at the designated place and, as he got out of the car, Georgie would say, 'Drive around for half an hour, Victor, and then pick me up.' Then he would disappear into the building.

Of course all this was reported back by me to the mysterious men working for the British Secret Service – I never found out who they were. MI5? MI6? All they ever said to me was, 'Don't worry about it, Victor – you're doing a great job.' I often had visions of rows of dusty pigeon-holes in which my contributions to national security had ended up. Perhaps they are still there.

After a bit Georgie had complete confidence in me. On our trips to the trade delegation it would be, 'Come, Victor, lunch and a drink or two.' Together we walked in to be greeted by everybody there as if we were a normal part of the outfit. The big chief in charge at the delegation had a name that I was quite unable to pronounce. It began with a 'B' so in order to make things easier I called him 'Britvic'. I don't think he ever cottoned on. This individual was a huge man, weighing in at around twenty stone. In moments of special jubilation, he used to greet me by slapping me on the back with such force that if I hadn't been prepared he could have sent me flying into outer space. Britvic was the big noise, KGB to the core and a real crony of Georgie boy.

It was at one of these lunchtime gatherings that Georgie tapped me up about the Chinese caper. They wanted someone who was unknown to the lad I was to keep a check on and rather too quickly I agreed to play the part. The way I looked at it, what they were suggesting could only make life more interesting and so long as I watched out for myself I would be OK. I did wonder about getting in my two mysterious sponsors from British security but I had no address for them and no way of getting in touch. Anyway, I thought it might be to my advantage to tell them after it was all over. The last thing I wanted was to

have my Russian employers finding out that I was involved
with sources they might not approve of. I thought about
the lessons Popski had drummed into me all those years
ago in the Western Desert. One of the things he insisted
on was, 'If you're working on your own, make sure that
you are indeed alone.' I was happy to help Georgie and his
friends out. It would be an interesting sideline but it
would be on my terms.

As well as driving Borovitch all over the place, I was
expected to take Cherny to the big receptions at the embassy;
this was a new departure for him: in the past he had stayed
away from such functions. Cherny's wife enjoyed all the
razzamatazz, but I had the feeling that Cherny himself
would have been happier sitting at home with a bottle of
vodka and smoking his favourite coffin nails. These late
nights at the embassy were still part of the routine, and
they continued to upset Freda. To calm her down I told her
that I would have a word with them, say something like, 'I
think you should get yourself a new driver'. But I didn't
actually do anything; for the time being I wanted to keep
all my options open.

The next time the men from the ministry made contact
I decided to have it out with them. I wanted to know who
I was working for. I asked them if there was any sort of
insurance policy. 'What do you mean, insurance?' 'Just
suppose they catch on. All I will know is that one fine
morning Cherny will say, "Victor, go embassy", and having got there that's the last anyone will see of me on
English soil. Surely you don't suppose that I don't know
the score.'

One of them turned to me. 'Keep the game going,
Victor. What you've told us so far is small stuff, but it is

very promising. I'll tell you this, Victor, when certain people read about that little escapade in Regent Street, they will get up on the table and start dancing. You have their confidence. They need people like you the same as we do. We'll have a good talk when we get back to the office, let them know your worries. Mark my words, Vic, you've got access to the trade delegation and that's where it all happens. One of us will pop round in a couple of days and tell you what we've sorted out.' They handed over an envelope that contained twenty quid and with that it was goodbye. I was left ruminating about possible escape routes if things went upside down.

The next day I didn't turn up until the afternoon, which meant Cherny had to make his own way to the bank by taxi. He was livid and went for me like a dog after a bone. He made me cart him straight round to the delegation and once he was inside he started a battle royal with Georg. The noise could be heard even by me sitting outside in the car. When Cherny finally came out it was obvious that he had been put in his place by some higher authority. Back at the bank Cherny got his secretary in to explain to me that in future all my orders had to come from him. I was to ignore any orders from Comrade Borovitch.

I began to acquire more duties. The Russian Embassy staff usually needed special permission to travel outside a fifteen-mile radius of London, but in this case the British Foreign Office gave special dispensation to use a house at Hazlehurst in Kent as a weekend retreat. I used to take a party down on the Saturday, leave them and then pick them up on the Sunday. Needless to say, the house was set back inside its own grounds, away from the eyes and lenses of the press that were always sniffing around.

One Friday night Chernuzube told me that he was going to Hazlehurst on the Sunday morning. I was to pick him up at eight sharp. I arrived bright and early and Cherny said we were to stop at the trade delegation on the way which was just a few yards up the hill. It was no more than an oversized two-storey house, set well back in its well-wooded hideaway and surrounded by a ten-foot wall with a pair of massive iron gates to the front. Only the resident security staff and the director lived in the building; all the rest of the odds and sods had rooms in the surrounding area. If they were outside walking distance they would catch a bus or the Underground, just like any ordinary worker.

This, of course, did not mean that they were free to roam at will after working hours; not for them to enjoy a walk around the local park in the cool of a summer's evening. If by some chance they were absent from their lodgings and a member of the British security staff paid them a visit, they had a lot of explaining to do. These Russian workers were kept on a very short leash.

Anyway, we duly picked up three of his compatriots, including Britvic and another heavy who was massively built but quite jovial. Then off to Hazlehurst, where they spent the day getting tanked up. By six o'clock, when it was time to come home, they were well past the walking the white line test; in fact, they would have needed the whole road. I wasn't exactly sober myself, but at least I could see straight. We were in the suburbs of London when Cherny told me to stop at the next eating house, which was quite unusual.

Out of the car they staggered, all four of them giving forth in song, no doubt about the glorious Motherland. I sat in the car and prepared for a long wait. The establishment they had gone into was owned and run by a Polish family and the clientele were 90 per cent Polish, who did not like the Russians at all. I heard shouting and thought that perhaps all was not well with my charges. So in I went. Chernuzube had his coat off and was shouting at the Poles, who in turn were calling the Russians the scum of the earth. As I opened the door Chernuzube was knocked to the deck. Apparently the Pole at the counter had refused to serve them.

With great difficulty I managed to get three of them out and into the car and then went back for Britvic who was holding the enemy gang at bay, and together we beat a retreat. The experience must have sobered them up because the rest of the journey was completed in silence. I was told to keep quiet about the whole affair, but it must have got around the delegation because when I went there two days later I was slapped on the back, vodka was put on the table and I became so drunk they had to send another driver to pick up Cherny. From that time on, as far as Brivic was concerned, I could do no wrong.

I had been at the bank for about ten months and life seemed to get more exciting by the day. By this time I could read Cherny like a book. He had his 'happy face', which meant that all was right with the world, and what I called his 'ulcer face'. He suffered from stomach ulcers and in the morning when he left his house grimacing with the pain of it, everyone knew to keep well clear. One morning, as I brought the car to the door, he emerged with a face like thunder. 'Victor, we go embassy ten o'clock, not be late.' That was the limit of Cherny's English, but it was enough. It was my responsibility to make sure that we arrived dead on time. Being late for a

meeting with the big man at the embassy was not on the
cards. The boss there was not the ambassador but a KBG
controller called Suslov. At exactly 10 a.m. I anchored up
in the grounds of the embassy in Kensington Park Road.
Cherny shot straight into the big, forbidding building
and I waited, sitting in the car reading Cherny's *Financial
Times*. I think he only carried this paper for show; even
after eight years at the bank his knowledge of English was
about as good as my knowledge of Russian, which is to say
almost non-existent. Suddenly, one of the embassy heavies
tapped on the car window and signalled me to follow him.
We went through the kitchens and into the staffroom
where a table was laid with mouth-watering delicacies
and a bottle of Stolichnaya to wash everything down. I
was given a warm welcome, with a lot of backslapping
from the heavies as they tried out their English on me. I
wondered what it was all about. I was soon to learn.

After a bit a woman came down, escorted me up the
back stairs to the top floor, where I was ushered into a
small room and greeted by Borovitch. He introduced me
to a small, slightly built individual whose name I couldn't
twist around my tongue. Comrade Borovitch opens up:
'Victor, we are going to ask you if you are willing to per-
form certain duties for us. You will still be employed by
the bank but sometimes you will be working for the trade
delegation. We are not going to ask you to inform on your
countrymen or do anything illegal. We admired the way
you carried out the operation at the Chinese Embassy.' I
was not completely surprised by this request; what worried me was that this was all taking place inside the
embassy. Up to this point I thought the embassy was the
Soviet government's open face to the British public. It was

the trade delegation building that I associated with under-cover chicanery. I also knew that if I agreed to what they were suggesting there was no way I could go on claiming to be a chauffeur to the chairman.

I started wondering about a new wage structure, but first of all I needed to know just what they wanted me to do. I was certain that Borovitch was working for the trade delegation and that his office at the bank was just a cover for his illegitimate operations. I was his bagman, carrying the cash for him in broad daylight, just as I had been doing for Popski all those years ago, the only difference being that if Popski and I had been caught by the enemy that would have been the end of it. Borovitch went on talking and I realised I would have something interesting to report to the men from the ministry when they next deigned to show up.

But then the pair from British security who had been keeping in touch with me suddenly disappeared from the frame. Their place was taken by several men and a woman. They used to appear without warning, usually when I was polishing the car. They always asked the same questions: was there anyone new doing business with the bank? Had I picked up any new arrivals at the airport or the docks? How was I getting along with my masters? The usual chat, the usual answers. They told me to carry on noting the addresses and said what I was doing was of great importance and inter-est to the powers that be. I was given an address in Rathbone Place, off Oxford Street. 'Don't post the reports, drop them in the letterbox, no need to enter the building.' I sensed trouble ahead.

One morning, after I had been at the bank for just over a year, I was called into the chairman's office and out of the

blue told: 'Victor, tomorrow you go out and buy Cadillac!' I
asked his secretary to explain what he meant: 'He just wants
you to go out tomorrow and buy a Cadillac.' I said, 'If he
expects me to cart him around London at the speed of light
in a Cadillac, tell him to think again.' I had learned by now
that the only way to carry on a conversation with Cherny was
to give it to him straight from the shoulder, no beating about
the bush. I explained that if I took a corner at anything like
the speed he was accustomed to, the car would turn over, and
in any case Cadillacs were too big and heavy for London
traffic.

It turned out that what was really getting to him was
the fact that one of his comrades, who was in charge of the
Baltic Shipping Line, had recently acquired a Rolls Royce
Silver Dawn. Cherny, feeling no doubt that the bank was
far more important than a mere shipping line, wanted
something bigger. So I said, 'Leave it to me and let's see
what I can come up with.' As luck would have it, the
garage where I kept the Humber, up in Highgate Village,
had been trying for some time to offload a Mark 7 Jaguar
because the new Mark 8s had just arrived, and needed
space in the showrooms.

That evening I approached Mr Silver, the owner of the
garage, and opened negotiations.

'How much in my hand if I can get a sale?'

'Sixty pounds,' he said.

'Not enough, make it a hundred.'

'Settle at eighty then.'

We struck the deal over a couple of pints in the pub next
door. He was happy, I was happy, and the guv'nor would get
the ride of his life. So the next day I reported to Cherny that I
had just the car for him. 'Go and get it.' He baulked a bit at

the colour – he wanted black and the Jag was a really grotty sandy colour – but when he settled down for the ride home, all the blue lights lit up on the dashboard and the beast accelerated off, he was sold. And, of course, I knocked six minutes off the journey. 'Good,' he says, which meant that he liked it. I also liked it when I went to collect my eighty quid.

One day there was an almighty row going on in the chairman's office – Cherny and Georgie were going at it hammer and tongs. The next morning I was called into the office and told that I now must purchase a car for Mr Borovitch. Once more I trotted up to Silver's Garage. 'Got anything else you're finding it hard to move?' Mr Silver showed me a Standard Vanguard. 'I can only allow you forty pounds on this one.' 'I'll be back in two days,' I said. 'Have my forty quid ready.' Once Georgie had his own car, I didn't drive him much any more, which was a relief.

There were six Russians including the chairman's secretary employed at the bank; they must all have been experts in their field. What Chernuzube's field was remained anybody's guess. I reckoned that it was his job to keep everybody in line, which he was good at. I don't think he liked his bank being used as cover for Russian intelligence. The bank had twice been raided by MI5, but on neither occasion was anything incriminating found. The British spooks withdrew with their tails between their legs. The chairman left the running of the staff to the two senior British employees, the secretary and a woman who served as the treasurer. Both of them professed to be long-standing members of the Party, and both of them, I was certain, were passing on information to a British Intelligence source. Georg Borovitch once confided in me that they had known about these two for years but had decided to leave them in place. I remember that Popski once told me that if you found a traitor in your midst, it was better to keep him tied to his job rather than shoot or sack him. 'Eliminate a known enemy source,' he said, 'and then you have the problem of identifying his replacement.'

The Russians did their service abroad in five-year stints, then they were replaced. Chernuzube had finished his first five years and then worked the double shuffle to get him and his wife another five years. You didn't need a university degree to understand that not many of them really looked forward to going back to the Motherland, not after tasting the delights of living in the west.

Saturday 25 February 1956 was the last day of the Twentieth Congress of the then USSR. It was on this day that Khrushchev, the big chief of all the Russians, opened a can of worms by talking about the man the Russian people hailed as their liberator from the Nazis, Comrade Stalin no less. Khrushchev made a speech that lasted six hours, denouncing Uncle Joe. On the following Monday it was plastered all over the *Daily Worker*. The bank staff held a meeting in Chenuzube's office. The peace and quiet was shattered by the noise of heated discussion. The old man was steaming. I do not know what was said but when it came to knocking-off time all the senior staff climbed into the Jag. Up to then they had always caught the bus or got on the Tube.

All this happened during the week that I had arranged for the delivery of Georgie's new car. Unfortunately for the Russians lower down the ladder, the embassy smartly put the block on any more vehicles. There was much dark muttering. To the staff at the bank it seemed that Chernuzube was standing his ground to repel boarders. He was seen as the captain of the ship. Any newcomers not approved by him were viewed as interlopers. Once the eruption caused by the Twentieth Congress died down he got on with the job of reasserting his authority. His crown had slipped to some extent, but, like all the rest of the old-timers, Cherny knew his way around the system.

The next sensation to hit the Russian fraternity came when the Soviets invaded Czechoslovakia. From then on it became part of my duty to protect Cherny from being dragged out of the car every time we visited the embassy. There was an almost permanent camp of dissidents gathered at the gates in Kensington Park. Any car trying to get in had to wait while the gates were opened, and when it was stationary the crowd tried to get at the passengers. I used to get out of the car, defying anyone to do their worst. I was a big, strong bloke and, thanks to the army, I knew how to handle myself. I always got Cherny through. The worst thing to happen was a brick thrown through the windscreen. There was always the possibility of physical injury to someone but not from me; damaging demonstrators was not part of my game even if they were trying to injure the people they hated. The police only made half-hearted attempts to keep the mob at bay, and some of the more witless elements ended up on the bonnet of the Jag. Cherny just sat in the back of the car and snarled at them as they banged on the windows. It was all part of the fun and games. When the gates opened I just carried on until I braked in front of the embassy. Anyone clinging to the car was heaved off by the heavies who hung around on guard for just such an emergency.

Another place I was sent to a lot was Berolina Travel in Conduit Street, near Piccadilly. This was the travel agency which dealt with all visas and travel arrangements for the German Democratic Republic. As far as I could make out it was a bona fide business. The GDR had never been recognised by the British government, who considered it to be an illegal regime, and as a result there was no representative of the GDR in Britain. Berolina partly filled the gap.

I had now been at the bank for more than two years and for most of that time I had sailed close to the wind. If my employers discovered that I was passing information about Georgie and the rest of the goings on at the trade delegation I would have been for it. But I wasn't ready to quit. It wasn't money that kept me at it; I could have earned the same driving lorries up the Great North Road for any one of the dodgy firms who were still plying their trade and breaking every rule in the book. What I was doing for the bank, and the challenge it presented, gave me a big buzz. As I look back I realise how utterly stupid I was, yet again living a life that satisfied my ego, not caring or even giving a thought to the damage it was causing my family. Of course, in my sane moments I wanted nothing more than to return to the quiet life that all soldiers dream of: roses round the door and the wife and kids enjoying a happiness that was too good to be true.

Then the Russians invaded Hungary and the British Communist Party lost about a third of its membership. The Secretary of the Party, Harry Politt, resigned over the *Daily Worker*'s refusal to print the pro-Soviet report from their correspondent in Budapest. Harry Politt was basically a trade unionist who honestly believed that the welfare of the British working class was important. But Comrade Harry had one big fault: he believed Uncle Joe Stalin was infallible.

About two months after the Hungarian affair had quietened down I was told by Chernuzube to report to a Mr
Pavlov at the embassy. It turned out that one of their
chauffeurs had been sent home and they needed a spare
driver. Borovitch had suggested me. I said, 'But I'm
employed by the bank, not the embassy.' Pavlov told me
that the employment of any foreigner who came in touch
with Russian nationals was something that the embassy
oversaw. He was at pains to point out that I was not being
forced or coerced into taking on this temporary job, but
they needed somebody they felt they could trust. I made
the suggestion that, in their line of work, 'surely it would
be a better policy if you trusted no one'. This remark
seemed to satisfy him. For the time being I would attend
to the needs of Mr Chernuzube as usual but I might be
assigned to either the embassy or the trade delegation as
need arose. He also said that I should stay away from my
local Communist Party branch and cut all my connections
with the industrial side of the Party.

It was about now that I decided to write down everything I had learned in my three years at the bank. I
described everything I could remember, the events and the
people involved. I ended up with about twenty pages of
longhand, which I kept wrapped up in a package in the
boot of the Jag, waiting for an opportunity to hand the lot
over just as soon as the next contact broke cover. What
would happen if Borovitch or any of the others had discovered
the package made the hairs on the back of my neck stand
up. It was almost three weeks before I got the chance to
get rid of this incriminating evidence of my perfidy, and,
luckily for me, Borovitch never had occasion to look in the
boot of the car.

I never asked myself why I had placed myself in such a precarious position. Except for the occasional envelope, with a couple of ten pound notes in it, I received nothing, not even a note of thanks, so why was I doing it. I suppose it was because I liked living on the edge, whatever the cost in terms of my family.

Freda and I decided that it was about time we had a holiday, so I bought an old wreck of a three-wheeled Reliant van for the princely sum of £10. This vehicle must have been at least twenty years old. The front wheel was attached to the steering column by a pair of old motorcycle girder forks, it was powered by an ancient Austin Ruby engine and the bodywork was made out of sheet aluminium. But at least it went along, although stopping the beast was a matter of luck. Luckily for me the MOT had yet to be invented.

Chernuzube gave me a fortnight off and I finished work on the Friday. After the dinner things had been washed and put away we all started packing the little Reliant. Into the back went our old army tent, along with all the other gear, the three kids sprawled out on top, buzzing with excitement. By nine that evening we had kissed goodbye to the Bourne Estate and were off on our journey to North Wales. With the kids singing their hearts out and the contraption lurching from side to side, we made our way northwards. Having managed Archway Hill and then Barnet Hill I began to have confidence that we might even make it to our destination, Criccieth.

We travelled all night and by morning we were nearing the area around Bala Lake. It was time to stop. We unloaded, got the tent up, and in broad daylight, in between the road and a railway line, we all lay down to get a few hours' kip. The stop lasted two days. The next morning I took Alan walkabout and discovered a small lake complete with water-fall, which is where Judith learned to swim. I jumped off a rock, about twenty feet above the water with Judith in my arms. The kids loved it, but Freda was worried about the safety of her brood and gave me some real stick.

On we went and at last we made it to a place called Blackrock. We pitched the tent at the bottom of the cliff edge. Freshwater bubbled from a hole in the rock face and the public toilets and wash-houses were only a hundred and fifty yards away. The main promenade of this small North Wales village was just around the bend in the cliff. We were completely on our own and it was as near to heaven as it was possible to get. After the first three days all the tensions that had built up because of my mishandling my responsibilities disappeared. Freda and I had found each other again. It got to be so hot that I cut the sides of the old Reliant open with a tin-opener. By the time we finally made it back to base on the Bourne Estate the Reliant, which had struggled to main-tain its dignity throughout the trip, gave up the ghost. It was sold to a lad for £10, so we lost nothing and we had enjoyed a gem of a holiday.

Being completely divorced from the routine at the bank, as well as the self-induced pressures, I had time to think about the enormity of what I was letting myself in for. I was beginning to understand the nature of the game I was sucked into and I decided that it wasn't to my advantage. A few quid followed by a pat on the back by both sides? No. I decided I would have a few words with the men from the ministry, ask for my cards at the bank and get out while the going was good. That break in North Wales had given me an insight into what life could be like and I did not want that to end.

When I reported back to the bank Cherny was all smiles. They had taken on a temporary chauffeur in my absence, a smart looking lad of about fifty who was forever prancing on about the fact that he was 'Rolls-Royce trained'. To give him his due, the Jag looked a whole sight cleaner and more polished than when I had it, and Cherny was highly impressed by having the car door opened for him as he got in and out. What I didn't tell the new lad was that while he was getting just over £40 a month I was clearing over a hundred. Evidently the 'Rolls-Royce training' didn't include any serious wage bargaining.

Although I had decided to finish with the job as soon as possible, as the weeks progressed and the work resumed its normal routine, somehow I never got round to giving it the drop kick. I had come to an arrangement with the new chauffeur: I would pick Cherny up in the morning, and take him home, and the new boy would fill in with the late nights and whatever overtime was on the cards, which he jumped at. Cherny quickly realised that his new chauffeur, who was so good at opening doors, was not so clever at getting him through the hostile mobs that hung around outside the gates.

9

An Enemy of the State

Nothing much happened for about two months and by now I was accustomed to the gentlemen of Fleet Street dogging my footsteps, asking for titbits of information but, as they offered me nothing, they got nothing in return. And even if they had been stupid enough to offer me a small reward for services rendered, they would only have been given some cock and bull story that I had made up.

For some reason good times never last with me. Borovitch was finding it difficult to park his car round central London to do his dirty work. So Chernuzube told me that I was to drive him again. Georgie was all smiles and I made no objection as long as we didn't go back to the late-night routine. I got to know a lot about what he was doing, his contacts in London, what they did for a living, and how often they met. When you think that Georgie, a sort of Soviet spy, was being followed at every twist and turn by me, a representative of the enemy, it was a gift from the gods for my sponsors in the British Secret Service.

Before we got going Georgie gave me a warning. He said that if I was told to do a job at the trade delegation I was to keep my eyes in the rear-view mirror and if I thought I was being followed I was to turn round and go straight back. 'If

anybody tells you to do otherwise then refer them to me or
Mr Popov at the embassy.' He went on to talk about things
in general. 'I will tell you something, Victor. If I get tum-
bled the worst that can happen is that I will be deported
back to Moscow, but if they get some idea that you're
involved you will spend the rest of your life in prison.' We
were chatting away as if we were old mates in the pub after
a day's work. I told him that I was never going to do anything that posed a danger to my country, and as for the
Soviet Union I didn't give two monkeys about what happened over there. But I got the point: Georgie was telling
me to watch my back.

Borovitch was a good-looking bloke and he was having it
off with Cherny's new young secretary. One day he asked me
if I could help him get hold of a small flat somewhere close.
As a Russian he could not sign any of the necessary legal documents. The upshot was that Georgie's little love nest was
rented in my name and the two of them disappeared off to it
at infrequent intervals. Nobody else in the bank knew about
this arrangement and I thought, good on you, mate.

Borovitch could converse in flawless English, albeit with
that slight American twang. He also had a good command of
French. He carried a French passport, and he used this to
travel outside the area that he was meant to stay within. He
knew every trick in the book. One night, after a drinking
session, I took him home to our flat. I remember Freda saying, 'I could fancy that one.' I never let him near the house
again! Better safe than sorry.

I once asked him why he was in the spying business:
'Why are you doing all the dirty work for those bastards in
Moscow?' He told me he had studied at university and,
well, one thing led to another. 'I just follow the

instructions and keep my nose clean as far as I'm able.' He missed his two children but nobody but an idiot would want to go back. Sometimes he sat and raged at the evils of capitalism while at the same time admitting that the biggest evil of the lot were the incumbents of the Kremlin. How he kept sane was a mystery to me.

Sometime after this I was contacted by a woman; she was from our side of the fence. I guessed she was in her early thirties. Nothing much had happened and I had naught to offer, except to tell her that I urgently wanted a chat with somebody in authority. She seemed to be put out when she realised that I didn't recognise her as just that person, but huffily she said that she would try to arrange something. I told her to put it at the top of her agenda. After she had gone Borovitch came over and said he wanted me to take him to an address in Ruislip that afternoon.

We drove to the home of Morris and Lona Cohen, who lived in a double-fronted bungalow in Crawley Drive, Ruislip. The pair of them had entered Britain under the assumed names of Peter and Helen Kroger. They were part of the spy ring that passed information, stolen from the files of the Manhattan Project in America, to the Soviets. Peter Kroger's cover was that he was a bookseller. After meeting the Krogers I was sent down to Portland Bill to contact a man who I believe was a gentleman by the name of Houghton. I was to take him up to Ruislip, drop him off, then pick him up the next day and take him back to Portland. Long after I had left the bank the Krogers were arrested for spying and sentenced to twenty years in jail. Houghton got fifteen.

Time went by and I was chatting to some of the other chauffeurs in the car park when along came Borovitch.

'Where now?' I asked.

'Trade delegation.'

I hadn't seen Britvic for some weeks and he welcomed me with the customary big cheery grin and the usual mighty slap on the back, nearly knocking me to kingdom come. Britvic was by now the big chief of internal security at the delegation. First of all he asked me again if I was willing to work with them, and then he came straight to the point: this work meant keeping anything I did strictly to myself. If I did not wish to start this work I could go back to the bank and nothing more would be said. I was getting more than a bit browned off with the humdrum existence that I was leading. 'Tell me what you want,' I said and with those few words I propelled myself into a new life of intrigue and generally cocking a snook at the British Establishment.

My first job was to take a gentleman down to the South West, and when he had finished his business I was to drop him off as directed. This person had to be picked up at six the next morning from Purley, just south of Croydon. I told Freda that the early start was because Chernuzube had to meet a plane at London Airport, my first lie.

At the trade delegation Borovitch showed me an ageing Humber Super Snipe. The vehicle was not in the same class as the Jag but it had been garaged for the last three years and it was not on any British Intelligence list. On the journey, I remembered Borovitch's warning and kept my eyes on the mirrors until I was safely out of London and heading down the A3. I picked up the gentleman according to plan and took him to Portland. My orders were to drop him off outside the town so he could get a bus or a taxi in for the rest of the journey. After that I was to wait at a convenient café until he returned. He took about an hour, and then I drove him back to Kingston to drop him off at the house in Purley. As I took my leave that first time he dropped £20 into my hand. I was to visit this establishment time and time again.

My journeys with this person carried on at monthly intervals for six or seven months. Once we went right up north to Fraserburgh, on the far north-east coast of Scotland. We picked up a woman and dropped her near Rosyth, one of Britain's naval repair yards. If I ever needed confirmation that I was in work of a dubious nature, this trip gave it. I have to admit that I was revelling in the excitement of the work. Once again I was back in the groove that seemed to suit me, of living on the edge. A couple of times the couriers, as I believe they were, turned out to be women. On another occasion, I noticed a black Humber keeping its distance. It followed us right on down the Portsmouth road, through Esher. I got as far as Bagshot and then pulled into a transport café that I knew. We went inside and sat down.

'Nothing doing,' I said to the passenger, 'I'm turning back.'

'What on earth for?'

I pointed out of the window of the café, and there, sure enough, was the Humber. The passenger went as pale as a ghost. After drinking our tea we headed back the way we had come, no doubt to the annoyance of the lads who had been tagging us. When I told Georgie what had happened he simply said, 'Glad you remembered'.

At this stage I was still in the habit of writing everything down, which meant that whenever the security people contacted me at Finsbury Circus all I had to do was pass the envelope to them through the window of the Jag. This took seconds rather than the half-hour or so it had taken to describe everything verbally when I first started the job. The spooks seemed content with these slapdash methods. There were times when I felt really at risk carrying information I had jotted down. There it all was filling up the inside pockets of my jacket. And, of course, if I was found out I could be in big trouble. Once inside the embassy I was effectively in Moscow and no British authority could help me.

The next time I was called to the embassy I mentioned to Popov that in future I would prefer it if someone came with me, preferably one of his staff. He didn't take too kindly to me attempting to lay down the rules but admitted that he could see my point of view. If risks were to be taken they would have to be in on it. The way I saw it was that if a crisis occurred I could rightly claim that I was carrying out my employment as a civilian driver for the embassy. I wasn't called on for another six weeks.

Reporting all these goings-on to the gentlemen from MI5 I was told simply to carry on and to do nothing that might cause my employers to suspect that I was two-timing them. For the first time they handed me the sum of £200, 'to be going on with'. This was a lot of money in those days and I willingly took it; if one side or the other or, as in my case, both sides, wished to pay me a bit on the side for playing a very minor part in their fantasies, that was fine by me.

Things were hotting up. I used to pick up Chernuzube and two or three of his staff in the morning. By the time I reached Kentish Town I would have a tail, a Humber, which followed us all the way to the bank. They were well and truly on to the Jag. One morning the guv'nor's ulcer must have been playing him up something awful. He told me to pull up as we were going down York Way, approaching King's Cross. He jumped out and went back to the tailing car and started a slanging match with the occupants. It must have shaken them up a bit as they turned around there and then. They didn't follow us again.

Sometime in 1956, Georgie's habit of charging about here, there and everywhere came to an abrupt halt. He told me later that, because of the uproar in the British press over the disappearance of Buster Crabbe, who had vanished in Portsmouth Harbour while spying on a moored Russian warship, it had been decided from higher up that all clandestine operations were to close down until everything died down.

I learned that a new man had appeared on the scene. I was summoned to the embassy and ordered to take this individual to a reception at the Bulgarian Embassy that evening. Suddenly, in walked Borovitch; he had bags under his eyes like coal sacks. He must have been getting his money's worth out of the secretary. 'I will be there, Viktor, and you will be introduced to a few people you may have to meet in the future.' The alarm bells were beginning to ring once more, but the way I looked at it, in for a penny, in for a pound. Once again I agreed to go through with whatever was in the offing.

At the reception I was introduced to three men and a woman. I am quite certain that they didn't know each other. Georg, leading the guests around the room, stopped beside me: 'I would like you to meet "Viktor"', and Viktor would give a nod and then retire back to a seat near the bar, where I did not drink anything. Getting myself even a wee bit merry wasn't on the cards. I was only there for the introductions.

It remained my policy never to get overly familiar with these people. I kept my conversation to a basic 'yes', 'no', 'how' and 'when'. Once more Major Peniakoff's advice came back to me. During my days chasing around the Western Desert he had given me a short lecture on how to keep alive while carrying out covert operations. 'Keep as far as possible in the background, never bring attention to yourself, never wear clothes or do anything which may bring you to the attention of any bystander; if possible, never let your right hand know what your left hand is about to do.' Timely words of advice that I was now putting to use.

Over the next few months I met a lot of people, and they weren't all from the ranks of the British proletariat. Georgie asked me to find some meeting places where I could make contact without drawing attention to myself. I came up with the old Tatler News Theatre in Charing Cross Road, a working man's café close to South Kensington Tube station, and, of course, the old reliable Lyons Corner House in Leicester Square. I also introduced Georgie to the restaurant in Swan and Edgar, the big department store right on the corner of Piccadilly Circus. The beauty of Swan and Edgar was that the restaurant was on the first floor directly facing the entrance to the store. I could easily get a table overlooking the main entrance and if I sensed that all was not well I had a convenient escape route down the back staircase leading to the emergency fire doors which were never locked. When I introduced Georgie to Swan's he almost choked with delight. 'Perfect' was the word he used. Borovitch or one of his henchmen would set up the meet. I would make the contact, collect whatever had to be passed on, go home and pass the envelope or package to Georgie the next morning.

I was involved in a right cat-and-mouse game with a group of about six men, all of whom I recognised by sight. I was instructed to act in any manner that I saw fit in order to keep everybody's trust.

If I was to make a rendezvous, at, say, three in the afternoon, I got into position at least an hour beforehand. The drill was that when I was satisfied that all seemed to be in order I made myself known to the courier, and no one else. I made it clear to my friends from MI5 that while I was prepared to give them advance notification of these pickups, if they wanted to carry out any surveillance the men they employed had better be very discreet, and that if I spotted them the meeting would be off. To my surprise they agreed with me. 'Carry on the way you're doing, Viktor, you're doing well.' By now I was hardly ever in the bank. I was working almost exclusively for the embassy and the trade delegation.

One evening I nearly got my comeuppance. One of Georg's compatriots had passed the word along that I was to meet a gentleman in the Strand Palace Hotel. This was not at all to my liking. I didn't know anything about the venue, I had not met the contact and to cap it all in the last couple of months both sides had increased their surveillance on me. I was also looking for a way of extricating myself from the whole business. The only person I felt I could trust was Borovitch. Unfortunately for him, his wife had appeared from Moscow, and being a woman it didn't take her long to suss out that her beloved was supplying Cherny's secretary with what she naturally believed was rightfully hers. The well-worn mattress in the flat was put into retirement, and I handed the keys back to the couple on the ground floor who were the landlords. Georgie was in disgrace and shoved on the sidelines for about a month so I had nobody to turn to. Against my better judgement I agreed to the meeting.

The only information I had was that the individual would come through the door at 7 p.m. precisely, and that he was short in stature. That afternoon I visited the place. I didn't like what I saw: there was no route through which to beat a hasty retreat if this became necessary.

As was my custom I was in position at six o'clock. By 6.30 two different tables, just inside the foyer, had been taken by two couples, and at 6.45 another two gentlemen arrived. To my way of thinking the suits they were wearing were just that bit too neat and tidy; the giveaway was the tie that one of them was sporting: Royal Artillery. The pair of them stood out a mile. There was a woman who didn't seem to fit in either. How often would a woman on her own walk into a large restaurant and sit down without ordering anything? It was obvious as they glanced in my direction that they knew I was there. It looked to me as though the meeting was being covered by the Russians as well as the British. If I was right the group that had been sent from the trade delegation would want to know why I was being ignored by British Intelligence. The answer would have been as plain as a pikestaff: this Victor, so trusted by the embassy, was playing a double game.

I knew that the game was up. I had to get out, and as soon as possible. I paid the waiter for the four cups of coffee that I had drunk and calmly walked out. No attempt was made to stop me. I walked up Aldwych, up Kingsway, in and out of the Underground at High Holborn and within half an hour I was indoors, deep in thought and shaking like a leaf.

The following morning I went straight to the delegation and had a chat with Borovitch. I told him what had happened and said that I thought I was being used as bait by one side or the other to get at the real villains of the piece. Back at the bank I got a message from Georgie saying that it had been agreed it would be better if I continued my normal work until things quietened down. I couldn't have agreed more.

However, it was not to be. I was sitting in a café in London Wall having a nice cup of coffee, getting used to having nobody breathing down my neck, when one of the bank's messengers burst in. 'You're wanted in the office straightaway, Vic.' Off I went, to find Borovitch with a couple of Russians I had never met before. 'Go straight home, Viktor, and tell your wife that you will be away for a few days. Report to the delegation in the morning.' No other explanation was given. Presumably all would be revealed the next day.

When I told Freda the news she was extremely upset, and that's putting it mildly. 'You mean to tell me that you're going away, and you can't even say for how long? I don't believe it. I thought we'd agreed that you were going to ease up a bit.' Once again, she was almost in tears. She probably thought I was having it off with a bit on the side. Perhaps I felt some pity, but if I did this was soon lost in the excitement of the operation. I was back where I wanted to be, on the edge, not caring that I was wrecking what was left of my marriage. All I cared about was me. The future lay in the cards. I had placed the bet without even seeing the cards I'd been dealt.

Next morning at the delegation I was ushered into one of the small conference rooms. Sitting around the table were six men, all Russians. Three of them I knew – Borovitch, Britvic and the chairman of the delegation – but the other three were new to me and were eyeing me up as if I had come down from outer space. Borovitch kicked off.

'First of all, Viktor, I must tell you that you will be operating on your own for a large part of this trip. If you agree to take it on you will have to exercise extreme caution. Also it

could put you in a very awkward situation should you be
picked up. If you wish to go ahead we will be in your debt.
If you wish not to you can leave now and, speaking person-
ally, I will not fault you for your decision. On the other hand,
if you stay in this room you will be committed. We will have
coffee while you give the matter some thought.' Over the
ensuing coffee there was much discussion among the six. At
one stage Britvic nearly came to blows with one of the other
three. Apparently this particular comrade had voiced some
doubts as to my integrity.

I didn't give it any thought at all. I said that I wanted to
speak with Georgie on his own. Outside the room I said,
'You realise, Mr Borovitch, that if I agree to whatever they
want me to do I'm being really stupid. If I get nailed they
might even put me in the Tower!'

'I cannot make up your mind for you, Viktor. I understand
that you've got a grudge against your government; we are
not going to ask you to give away any secrets because we
know that you haven't any to give. What they are going to
ask of you is a small task that it would be very difficult to do
ourselves – I don't see any danger in it.' This might not be
exactly what Borovitch said but it is near enough. We went
back into the room, I sat down and said, 'Count me in'.

It turned out that I was to take Chernuzube and Borovitch
up to St Andrews on the east coast of Scotland where Cherny
was giving a speech to a bankers' conference. From there I
was to take Borovitch up to Montrose, where I was to pick up
four individuals who were being landed from a fishing
trawler. Then I was to drive back, dropping two in Manchester
and taking the other two to London to the delegation. Silence
reigned in the room while I took in this information.

'What car am I going to use?' I asked.

'Well, the Jaguar, of course.'

I couldn't believe it. Presumably these men were all experienced in clandestine operations, and yet they wanted me to operate in a vehicle that was already under the scrutiny of British security. 'No go,' I replied, 'I want another vehicle, preferably hired, and, furthermore, no timetable. If you want me to carry on you must let me get them to the destination in any way I think fit. After all it's my neck.'

Borovitch translated my reply, after which more muttering, which ended in a burst of laughter from Britvic. 'What's the joke?' Georgie explained that they were saying that if anything went wrong I could always come to Moscow where I would be well looked after. I said, 'Tell them I would rather take my chances in Dartmoor than end up in some Soviet slave camp.' When the laughter had died down I said I would work out a plan of action and tell them about it the next day.

Then Britvic rang a bell, and in came one of their do-it-alls with a tray load of glasses and three bottles of vodka. This was followed by the usual sandwiches, and the meeting closed with much slapping of backs and handshakes all round. I went straight home to tell Freda that at least I wasn't going away just yet. Peace returned to the household.

That evening I sat down to do some serious thinking. First I had to make contact with my sponsors from British security. Apart from the address in Rathbone Place, I had no phone number and no other means of contact. I even thought about taking the risk of letting Borovitch in on what I was doing but decided against it, on the grounds that with Georgie, however much he railed against his masters, there would be no way he would put his family at risk. These men had underestimated me; they thought of me as someone they gave orders to and that I would do what I was told.

Then I thought about the four people I was going to pick up and assumed that they must have a fair grasp of the English language. I decided that it would be too risky having the four of them in the same car. I would take the two who were destined for Manchester to Inverness, where they could easily take a train with a minimum of risk. I would then go back to Montrose, pick up the other two, take them up to Aberdeen and put them on the train to York, where I would pick them up the following day. I also had to convince Borovitch that his presence on the exercise was unnecessary. And I certainly didn't want to use the Jag. This is what I told Georgie the next day and said that he could take it or leave it.

The next thing I did was to write down everything I knew about the coming operation. Freda wanted to know what I was writing about and I told her that I was just working out a possible route for this conference in Scotland. Georgie and I had a lengthy discussion about my proposals; he wasn't too keen on being left out of it and doubted whether his superiors would agree. But he did admit that there was a lot of sense behind what I was thinking. Then he said, 'Let's go and have a coffee, Viktor', and that was it for the time being.

I kept turning the whole thing over in my mind, and I didn't like the conclusions I came to one bit. If it went wrong I might find that I had no friends on either side. The stakes were too high; if the Russians did not agree with my conditions I was going to pull the plug and finish with the bank, full stop. On the family front all the so-called early nights and more time together that I thought I would get when I started had never materialised. Some nights it was nearly dawn before I walked through the front door. Freda was being tested to the limit. Maybe I should call a halt anyway. For the first time I was at a loss, but in the end I decided to stick with it, shit or bust.

The next day found me with Mr Silver.

'Looking for another car, Vic?' he asked, scarcely able to restrain himself from rubbing his hands together as the prospect of a sale crossed his vision.

'No, I may want to hire a good-sized vehicle for up to a week.'

'No problem. What about the Princess?'

The Princess was a large coach-built job, one of the last of the big Austins ever made. It would have to do.

'If it comes off, add thirty quid to the charge as my bonus.'

'Come and have a drink.'

And, without further ado, off we toddle.

Two days later I was called into Chernuzube's office. 'Take tomorrow off, Viktor, get the car ready for the trip to St Andrews. We shall be leaving on Monday. Can we do it in a day?'

Thinking of Cherny's ulcer and the fact that we would not be going in the Jag, I answered in the negative. This didn't please him one bit so when I suggested that if he wanted to do the trip in one go we would have to leave at four in the morning, he agreed. As I came out of the chairman's office I found Borovitch waiting for me. We went to our usual café in Moorgate where I gave him an update.

'Chernuzube thinks we're going in the Jag.'

'Don't worry about it,' says Georgie. 'Have you arranged for another car?' I told him about the Princess. He told me that I had been overruled about going it alone. He would be coming up to Montrose with me. I left him sitting in the café with a worried look. I had the feeling that his usual self-assurance was slipping. Later I picked up the Princess and went home for the weekend.

On Sunday I walked to Rathbone Place to drop in a letter, only to discover that the door was covered in dust. Builders were in: the house was deserted. I came home with the note still undelivered. I was going into this operation without back-up. There could be problems.

On Monday morning, sharp at four, the Princess was purring outside Cherny's house on West Hill. Out they all came, Cherny leading the way followed by the overscented secretary, another Russian who was new to me, and, bringing up the rear, my mate Georgie. In they all piled, with the secretary sitting in the front seat. 'Where's the Jaguar, Viktor?' 'Not fit for the journey, guv, the brakes are dodgy.' The fact that the Princess was a nice gleaming black seemed to placate him, because he lit up one of his favourite fags and off we shot, heading north. We rolled into St Andrews at nine in the evening. After attending to the luggage, off I staggered to my room for a good night's kip.

Montrose is a typical small fishing port, able to handle coastal traffic and the occasional medium freighter that finds it more convenient to use small ports rather than the larger ports like London and Liverpool. These ports, which are dotted round the coast, are small enough for the local customs officers to lead a cushy life. Borovitch and I left St Andrews early the next morning and midday found us cruising round Montrose, looking for a suitable hotel, like a couple of tourists.

It was my opinion that if we were going to be watched by British Intelligence then they would put in an appearance the day after we arrived, by which time Georgie and I would be long gone. If we weren't there they would not know that they had missed us. Georgie and I went our separate ways the next morning. I had agreed to collect him and two of the agents from the fish market at four in the afternoon. I felt increasingly tense as the day wore on. I was in a strange town and didn't know whether the operation was going to work. Also, what we were doing was illegal. I think Georgie felt the same.

Right on the dot of four he turned up at the rendezvous point with two scruffy looking individuals, one Russian, the other French. 'Carry on with your original plan, Viktor.' After satisfying myself that the Russian's English was good enough to get him and his companion through the journey I left them to their own devices. I couldn't get away quick enough. So far so good.

I had already decided what to do next. Instead of returning to Montrose I left the car in the hotel car park and went to Aberdeen where I stayed the night. I then took a bus down to Montrose. Georgie boy could sweat it out for a few hours. I was playing it safe.

I got back to the hotel late that afternoon and found George having a severe attack of nerves. I told him that all I wanted to know was that the coast was clear. 'I'll get a coach back to Aberdeen at six tonight, you go back to the docks, bring the other two out and I will be back here by eleven. You can then go back to the hotel, have some sweet dreams and leave the rest to me.'

I couldn't really believe what was happening. Here I was telling the KGB how to carry out their operations. To my way of thinking they seemed to be as cack-handed as their British counterparts. In the end I didn't drop the two individuals at Aberdeen or York, as I had intended, but drove them directly to London, leaving them in a seedy hotel in King's Cross. I told them not to move until I came to pick them up the next day. Then I went to the delegation and told Britvic what had happened. I received the customary slap on the back. 'Pick them up now, Viktor, bring them both here.' Which I did and that was the end of my part in the operation. It was all too easy. I wondered whether it would be possible to get agents into the USSR with such ease. I doubted it.

All that remained for me to do was to make my report to my sponsors. But when I got to Rathbone Place, the foreman in charge of the work there said that all mail had been redirected to an address in Chenies Street.

When I got there I discovered that the new office was in an attic above a perfume manufacturer. Sod's Law again, the only soul there was a weary lady hammering away at a typewriter. I left her with a demand that somebody contact me as soon as possible. What worried me now was that I had been party to an illegal operation which could fall foul of the customs people and if they got involved they might take a different view of things to the intelligence people.

I had now worked at the bank for five years. Chernuzube had done his term and gone home, to be replaced by a new man called Andrey Dubonosov. The new man demanded that I open the car door for him like Barnet the other chauffeur did. I told him that if he wanted a lackey he should employ one, and hoped this would get me fired.

There was one last incident that finally persuaded me it was time to go. Borovitch had asked me to go to an address in Oxford to pick up a friend of his. He couldn't do it as he had other work to do, but he would meet the car outside Notting Hill Tube station at 7 p.m. Off I went to the address given, picked up the individual (who I knew because he was a well-known Member of Parliament), went down to Notting Hill and picked up Georgie, who then directed me to West Hill. By the time we were at Marble Arch I saw that we were being followed. Borovitch then said that on no account were we to carry on to the delegation; the two of them had to get out of the car somehow without being seen by our followers. I drove down Oxford Street, straight across Oxford Circus, until I got level with Wardour Street, then I jumped the lights, a quick right turn, into Wardour, then down through Bridle Lane (I knew the area like the back of my hand), out into Piccadilly Circus and I dropped them outside Leicester Square Underground station. The vehicle behind us just didn't stand a chance. Up to Hampstead Village where I put the Jag in the garage, jumped on my bike and made it off home as if nothing had happened.

When I told Georgie about my intention to leave the bank he agreed that it might be the best thing. It was obvious that I was getting too well known. Before I left, the Jag was sold off, to be replaced with a Rolls. Chernuzube would have revelled in it, but as a car it would never have served the same purpose as the Jag. During the last week of my employment, I was again approached by one of the well-dressed men who had been my shadow for the last couple of years. I was instructed to turn up in Chenies Street. Could I make it the following evening, around eight to eight thirty? It turned

out that they had only just become aware of the operation at
Montrose. I gave them a full description of the individuals,
the times and dates.

'Was it your impression that these men were important?'

'Not to my way of thinking, just foot soldiers.'

'What gives you that impression, Mr Gregg?'

I was very tempted to reply that they seemed to me to be
just as stupid as their opposite numbers, but for once discre-
tion ruled the day.

'That's my thinking,' I replied, which seemed to satisfy
them until I dropped the bombshell. 'I'm leaving next week.
I've decided that enough is enough.'

The chap who appeared to be the senior of the two came
back at me. 'Why don't you hang in a bit longer? It could be
that there might be something right up your street we can
offer you.'

I didn't even give it a second's thought. 'No thanks. As
I've said, I'm out.'

I had been of considerable use to them, right inside the
enemy fortress, trusted by the embassy, a difficult act to
replace, but in spite of their pleading I remained adamant.
I'd had enough. 'What, after that song and dance you led
us the other night?' I just grinned at him, he saw the light
and wished me Godspeed. I left with the knowledge that
I must have contributed in some small measure to the
conviction of at least half a dozen of these so-called enemies
of the state. The Portland spy ring was finally rounded up
just after I left. Whether or not the titbits of information
that I supplied concerning the Krogers and the half-dozen
or so others played any part in their eventual arrest I will
never know but I suppose it must have been of some
assistance.

So I left after what I can only say was an interesting and enlightening time. Freda was overjoyed: she was fed up with me never being at home, and I could never let on about what I was really doing. As far as she knew I was just working late. Much too late.

10

Goodbye, Bank

I left the bank sometime early in 1962. Freda and I were still living on the Bourne Estate, but we had been offered a new flat on an estate in Roehampton. Our marriage was battling to survive. Perhaps we could make a fresh start; we were grasping at straws, but if I could manage to turn over a new leaf it would be well worth the upheaval.

My involvement with the Communist Party was dwindling, but soon after I left the bank I was summoned to King Street (the Party headquarters) where a crackpot of a woman by the name of Betty Reid was attempting to lay the law down about one of the bank's employees. The row had been going on for some time.

Three senior English members of the bank, including Betty Reid, had been trying to find an excuse to get rid of an elderly woman, mainly because she was not afraid of speaking her mind if she disagreed with something. Over the months she had become quite a thorn in their flesh. It didn't help that this lady had been a well-known member of the Party before these two had left school. Knocking on fifty-eight, she was at times a bit slow with her work and her eyesight was beginning to show signs of wear. Anyway, there was a move to get rid of her. They put pressure on Chernuzube to dismiss her on the grounds that her work was not up to the standard of the others.

I had been involved in starting up a union for bank employees, the National Society of Bank Workers, and we were having some success recruiting members to our local branch. The long and short of it was that I was able to get a motion accepted that any attempt to oust this lady from the bank's employment would mean an immediate stoppage of work. That really put the cat among the pigeons and I was accused of being unfaithful to a socialist organisation. My reply was that the bank was carrying out trade in a capitalist economy, charging interest on loans to local councils which working-class citizens would have to pay for and so on. Borovitch saw my point, but Chernuzube didn't. I was too useful in other spheres and in the end Chernuzube closed the subject, giving a dressing down to the two heads of department responsible. When Betty Reid brought up the subject again, I just told her to jump in the lake, I was not going to get more involved. After that my name was mud.

My reputation was saved by the intervention of Bert Ramelson, the Party's main industrial organiser. Bert devoted his life to the service of the British working class and what's more he loved and was proud of his country's achievements. He didn't see eye to eye with Betty Reid and her tantrums. With Bert's help my reputation was restored. In breaking with the Party it wasn't that I had renounced my beliefs and suddenly seen the light; far from it. I realised that there was no way of getting rid of the British Establishment short of putting them all up against the wall, and I knew that such a thing was never going to happen, not in a million years. I was a realist and settled for the next best thing – I wanted to earn an honest living and repair the damage I had done to my marriage.

I tried to kid myself that I was doing all I could to keep us together, but in my heart I also recognised this was a lie. The

six wartime years of killing and keeping one step ahead of
the enemy in order to survive had passed by, but, alas, the
motor inside me was still running. My lust for new adventures and the desire to prove myself against the strength of
others was too strong. By now we had moved out of central
London and taken up the offer of the LCC for a flat in the
huge new housing estate in Roehampton, on the edge of
Richmond Park. Freda wasn't all that keen because all her
friends lived in the Holborn area, but I put in the idea that
it would be a better place to bring up the children – all the
fresh air of Richmond Park and beyond. There was also a
chance that the move away from my old stamping grounds
might help me sort out the mess I had made of things.

Moving to Roehampton had its drawbacks. There were
jobs, but the pay was pitiful. The two builders I approached
had a workforce that had been with them from the beginning of time, or so it seemed. No way was I going to earn the
money I considered I was worth in the leafy surroundings of
Roehampton. I spent two weeks traipsing around on the
lookout for a likely start. In the end I got in touch with some
of my old contacts with the result that I started work for
Hymie Rose, one of the biggest rogues in the British road
transport system. Hymie ran his business from the car park
at the rear of a pub on the edge of Greenwich Park. He had a
small fleet of ancient Atkinson semi-trailers, all of which
were powered by the equally ancient Gardner 5LW diesel
engines. Hymie's favourite saying was, 'I don't care who you
fiddle as long as it's not me'.

He thought it a disgrace to the industry if he paid for anything at full trade price. From fuel to tarpaulins, ropes, tyres
and even the trailers from twenty-five up to forty footers,
everything was bought on the fiddle. A fuel tanker would

back into the yard and Hymie would start haggling about how much he would give the driver for the surplus fuel he had fiddled by shortchanging the garages he had visited earlier in the day.

Hymie had a contract with south London's biggest steel reinforcement merchant, based in Battersea. The basic load we carried on our trips out of London was always ten to fourteen tons of steel reinforcement bars in sixty-foot lengths. The front half of the load rested on a welded steel bolster that supported it over the cab. The back end dangled over the back of the forty-foot trailer. Everything was held on to the trailer by chains. In this way we carried these dangerous and unwieldy loads to sites all over the UK.

Hymie also employed a couple of old lags whose job it was to take a load on one of the trailers that was well past its sell-by date. After delivering they parked up for the night on any of the big lorry parks that could be found all over the country. Then this pair of lads would calmly unhitch the old trailer and swap it for any decent looking empty trailer that had been left for the night in the park. And it wasn't just Hymie's little outfit that was on the fiddle; the big firms were at it as well.

To work for someone like Hymie it was necessary to have a skin like a rhinoceros. Being as hard as nails, he was not a believer in long drawn-out arguments about wages or conditions. Hymie was just as likely to remove his jacket, roll up his sleeves and invite the aggrieved driver to settle the argument in the backyard. Usually the other lads, knowing full well that the guv'nor was well past his best, would separate the two duellers and repair to the bar in the pub to sort out the dispute over a couple of pints. The drinks were always put on Hymie's tab. It was hard and it was brutal, but if you could do the job and stand the heat the rewards were as high as could be got.

The big standing joke about the firm's office was the notice on the door: 'Let it be understood that all drivers must produce a fully legal log sheet at the end of every working day'. The reality was that any driver producing even a scrap of paper resembling a log sheet would have been fired on the spot. The notice was there for the benefit of the road transport inspectors. Every now and then a firm would get done. Freda's brother-in-law worked for a business going by the name of Home Counties Transport; he was caught out when the inspectors went through the firm's fuel receipts. He got fined £500, all of which was paid by the firm.

You earned your money with Hymie by working all the hours that God sent. We didn't just deliver and come back to London empty; no, the name of the game was to make your delivery of reinforcing rods in whatever part of the country you had been sent to and then, as soon as you were unloaded, make a dash for the nearest big engineering area and find a load so you could drive back to London to deliver the next morning. A typical week's work started on Sunday night and ended on Saturday morning when you unloaded the stuff you had picked up on the Friday. Then it was down to the steelyard at Battersea to load up with more reinforcement rods for delivery on the Monday morning to any part of the United Kingdom. To survive you had to stand up to threats from any other driver who thought he had first call on the load you were about to take. Luckily for me I could look after myself. And so it went on, day after day, and of course there was no assistant to unload in London while you went home for a well-earned kip. One driver to one wagon, and if you weren't up to it, hard luck.

The reality of all this was that after I left home on a Sunday night I wouldn't see the wife and kids until the following Saturday afternoon. Not a recipe for keeping a marriage in good order. If I was going to play my part as a family man I had to get another job. I plucked up the courage to give the firm at Greenwich the drop kick and for a short time went back to Hamptons. I marched into their office on the off-chance that they might have a decent start on offer. I was told they had no fresh starts and that all the sites were fully manned, but after looking through my records, which all those big firms kept, they told me that they had a vacancy for a charge hand to keep the lads in order on a fair-sized job next to the Brompton Oratory. A charge hand was one rung down from the foreman, and being that one rung down meant that you had to do all the dirty work that the foreman didn't want to do. This included making sure that schedules were maintained, hours weren't fiddled and if it came to giving a lad his cards then it would be the charge hand who did it, including fighting him if he wanted to make something of it, and he often did.

Being a charge hand on a London building site was not a much-sought-after position, especially as the extra pay amounted to a measly three- or fourpence an hour. But it was that or nothing. When I got home that evening I told Freda that I had finally seen the error of my ways and that from now on I would try to be a pillar of society, and that I was now a charge hand at Hamptons. In the past we would have celebrated the new job with a trip down the local pub but with the three kids that was not possible.

The next morning I reported to the foreman on the site. The first thing he said was, 'I don't want to see you with a brush in yer 'and, your job is to keep this load of scruff 'ard at it. This job was in debt before we got on site and I got a clean

slate and I intend to keep it that way.' He told me that this
was a bonus job but the lazy sods hadn't earned any of it to
date. 'Don't forget you get your share of any bonus, so the
'arder they work the more you earn. Simple, mate, get 'em at
it. I'm off to the office now.' Then off he went, pedalling away
on his bike to the firm's building department office which
was situated in an alley off the lower end of Pall Mall.

This foreman, whose name was Riley, didn't turn up the
next day so I spent the time getting to know the 'lazy sods'
and trying to rectify the situation about the lack of bonus
earnings.

Riley turned up on the site the following Wednesday, by
which time I had the lads working in three teams. Before
my arrival they were each responsible for their own bonus;
there was no co-ordination on the job so they were all at cross
purposes with each other. By the end of the first week I had
sorted out the time and job sheets, signed them and handed
them over to Riley, who didn't bother to read them: 'Get
them down to the office.'

Mr Riley had been with the firm for years. He was regarded
by the management as a good, reliable employee, and they
took his word as gospel. My assessment of Tom Riley was
that, in his way, he wasn't a bad bloke, but being in his sixties
he had allowed the lads to ride over him, and once that was
part of the working routine all was lost as far as earning
decent money was concerned. On the Monday of the third
week we had a visit from the firm's senior general foreman
with one of the estimators of the job. They wanted to check
up on the work done in the last couple of weeks. 'How come
that all of a sudden the men are supposed to be earning all
this bonus?' I was told to report to the office. By the time I
had cleaned myself up, been down to the local café for a cup

of tea and a sarnie, I gets to the office and there they are eyeing me up and down.

'You've worked for the firm in the past, Mr Gregg.'

I had to admit that such was the case.

'Can you handle this job you're on now as a foreman?'

'Shouldn't be too difficult, providing I get the backing of this office on what things I think are necessary.'

Riley got transferred to another job and I took over in his place, which meant that I was on a monthly salary with no bonus. I thought this was stupid since it destroyed incentives but I fell in with it since I was determined to try to mend my ways and get stuck in with a 'normal job like other men do'. I knew that Freda would really have to convince herself that I was trying to make up for my past 'I don't give a monkey's' way of earning a living. One of the conditions I tried to impose was that as far as possible I kept the same crew together. Looking back on that episode of my life, I reckon that it must have been the sheer cheek with which I confronted these older men that got me through. After all, there was I, a relative newcomer, being offered a position that in many cases men had devoted their working lives to achieve, and to top it all, having the impudence to demand terms. How I got away with it I do not know. But I did and our little band of painters would arrive on a new job, go into a huddle and decide among ourselves the best method of screwing the firm for the maximum in bonus payments. What I had brought to this gang of men was no more than the standard procedure for operations in any Rifle Brigade platoon, and it worked.

Freda thought I had always got my way with my fists and although I did have periods when I went through life as peaceful as anyone could wish, but sooner or later my violence would break out. Sometimes I would come home in the evening to tell my Freda that I'd finished with the firm I was working for and she would merely remark, 'What, been fighting again?' Nine times out of ten she was correct. I was determined that this time things would be different.

Before a job started it was the custom for the office to call the foreman in to discuss the incentives 'to keep the lazy sods hard at it'. I took it upon myself to get the best deal possible from these men who, in most cases, didn't know the difference between a spade and a shovel. Our little band had got so organised that none of our jobs ever went into the red. Not only that, but word was going round that our bonus payments were going through the roof. The management must have decided that to have ordinary house painters earning more than the office staff was definitely not the right way to do things.

One week we started work on a big house at Lancaster Gate, the London abode of some lord, and he had the wealth to go with it. His wife had just returned from Paris where they also had a huge apartment. She didn't want ordinary paint to highlight the egg and tongue decoration on the ceiling cornices (egg and tongue was a type of plaster cornice decoration very popular in these big majestic town houses); no, she wanted gold leaf so gold leaf it had to be.

I went down to the office to explain that it was going to take that much longer to apply this gold leaf along about two hundred feet of egg and tongue. No problem, Mr Gregg, we have a specialist who does all the gold leaf jobs. I agreed to leave it at that and went back to tell the lads that we must expect to get held up on this job. I happened to know that the old boy who did these special jobs was in his seventies and would probably have to be lifted on to the scaffold from which he would be working.

Two weeks later the crunch came; the clerk of the works came round and explained that for some reason the job was behind schedule and falling into the red. 'How come your men are claiming bonuses when the job's almost at a stand-still?' 'It's the leaf work, guv, it's taken over the job.' The ceilings in this part of the property were about twelve feet high, and none of us, despite the old boy's rather superior attitude, wished ill of the old goat, but money was money and in our case it was floating out of the window. 'He's managing about ten feet a day, we can't do anything below him until he's clear, the chippies are still working in the other rooms, our progress is governed by the speed of the leaf, I should think it might be a good idea to have a word with the estimator.' The clerk of the works put on his coat and headed for the door saying, 'Nothing to do with me, it's been decided to stop any further bonuses while this job's in debt'. 'You're not meaning the payments we've already indented for?' ''Fraid so lads.' And off he went.

A voice spoke up. 'You get down there, Vic, and give it to 'em 'ard. No money no work. As for me,' the speaker continued, 'I'm off for the day.' And packing up his tools he did just that. The bloke was called Sid and was ex-navy. He was on HMS *Barham* in the Med when she got torpe-doed. Just before she sank beneath the waves she exploded into a million different pieces. 'You do that, Vic,' another of the lads pipes up. 'We're earning them a fortune, tell them what Sid just said, no money no work, we can drop this job and get another job tomorrow.' A couple of the lads were not too happy but they were out-voted by the other lads who were even less happy.

The next morning I'm down the office to have it out with the various men who lived under the impression that their word was law. 'You're the foreman on the job, Mr Gregg, you're still getting paid, what's it to you if we lay down the law to these men?' From that moment I knew I had finished with Hamptons. 'You're wrong, mate, those incentives were given by me, my word, nothing less, you either pay the men their due or you've lost probably the best working gang on your pay list. Including me. If you're not prepared to give way on this, bring round our cards and money before knocking off time tonight.' With that I marched out of the door down the outside iron staircase, jumped on my bike and made my way to the café round the corner from the job where I knew the lads were waiting.

I wasn't concerned about losing the job. It was Freda's reaction that worried me. She would see it as yet another example of my unstable nature when it came to keeping a job. I knew she would lay it on. If I wanted to stem the tide of scorn that was surely in the offing I had better think quick and come up with something earth-shaking, or at least some form of reliable employment. Right on the dot of five that afternoon round comes the pay clerk with all our cards and back cash; he said that any of us who wished to consider being re-employed could turn up at the office in the morning. This was a sop to the small number of older lads who had been with the firm for years and were considered to be reliable. So we said our goodbyes and we all went our different ways.

As for Sid, he had never fired a rifle or actually killed anyone in the six years of his service, but he was one of the few survivors from the *Barham* which went down with 840 of his shipmates. That single incident scarred him for life. He told me that he couldn't get away from the screams of his mates as they realised that they were locked in behind those heavy bulkhead doors with the sea rushing in and flooding their compartment. I kept in touch with Sid mainly because we got on well together, but he only lasted a year after the Hamptons affair. Sid was the nearest I ever came to having a friend who understood the power of those wartime memories and the misery that came with them.

I pedalled my way back home along the Brompton Road in the pouring rain, with my box of tools tied precariously to the back of the saddle, soaking wet from the rain that was coming down in torrents. In front of me was a bus with a big advert plastered all over the back of it informing all and sundry that a fortune could be made by any worthwhile man or woman who offered themselves for employment with London Transport as a bus driver or conductor. Not only that, but the advert went on about it being a job for life with a bright future and plenty of opportunity for advancement. All this and a pension scheme, too. I couldn't for the life of me think of a possible advancement up from a bus driver, except maybe an airline pilot. By the time I'd arrived at Roehampton my mind was made up. All problems solved. I'd decided that a trip to the training depot at Chiswick was the answer to my present predicament. There was no way out. I told Freda about the sudden loss of employment. 'But they've just made you up to foreman, they must have thought something of you.' There was cold air flowing in the flat that evening. I rose early the next morning and Freda got me a nice cup of tea. She was tired; I knew that she been awake most of the night and in any case was working all the hours God gave at her job in Wandsworth. She was helping to run a hostel for girls who had fallen foul of the law or were homeless, and I knew they all thought the world of her. She loved the work and would soon rise to being in charge.

London Transport took me on and I walked through the drawn-out three-week training session at Chiswick. Having passed the London Transport training session the squad then had to pass a driving test run by the government public service vehicles (PSV) office at Vauxhall. Out of the sixteen men who were put through the test only four of us passed.

The driving test for a PSV licence was much more stringent than an ordinary driving licence. After three weeks' training no faults were allowed; if, coming to a halt at a bus stop, the wheels of the bus were more than six inches from the edge of the kerb, you failed; cutting corners, failed; not applying the handbrake when stopping, failed. The list was endless. Nowadays it is simpler and easier. Finally I was granted the treasured PSV licence and detailed to present myself at Putney bus garage where I was introduced to the conductor I was to work with. We were told to do the 14 route, Putney to Hornsey Rise. The conductor was also a new boy. He had arrived in England less than three months earlier having been accepted for the job at the London Transport office in Barbados. Not only was I enjoying the job but I was getting along well with the lad I was working with. He was a well-built man with a habit of backing down if anyone tried to bully him because of his colour. The rest of the black drivers and conductors at Putney were mostly from Trinidad and there was bad feeling between the lads from Trinidad and the lads from Barbados. I could never work out why.

I I

Goodbye, Hamptons

It was now 1966 and for me it was all light at last. I was forty-seven. I liked the job, I was working on my own and as long as I kept to the schedule and turned up at the depot in good time to start my shift, what could possibly go wrong?

I soon found out. Freda never openly said that our earlier love was a thing of the past; after all, there were the three children who were the result of that love and we both in our own way doted on them. In her eyes, though, they could do no wrong and anyone who so much as whispered otherwise would be in for a severe going over. Freda was only following in the footsteps of her own mother and the thousands of other working-class mothers who believed that, whatever happened, you looked after your own, starting with the kids.

It was after a very noisy argument between us over this subject that Freda suggested that it might be better for both of us if we went our different ways.

'The boys are grown up and married now, Vic, I can easily look after Judith.'

'Are you talking about divorce?'

'Why not, Vic? Things are never going to get any better between us, it's not too late for both of us to make a fresh start.'

'Are you seeing another bloke then?'

'No, I'm not, although I'm not going to say that I haven't
had offers.'

'You know I started this job on the buses in order to make
up for things, surely you understand that?'

'Yes, I know what you try to do, Vic, but you've cried wolf
too many times and now the children are on their way in the
world. I want to make something of myself, Vic, I'm a wee
bit late to start a vocation, but that's what I'm doing now
and I know that I can do these young girls a power of good.
I suppose I will always love you, but it ain't working, you
know that. We try and it don't 'appen. Vic, just accept the
fact that it hasn't worked out. Think about it – time's running out for both of us.'

The truth of the matter was that way back in the past I
had committed the cardinal sin of having a short relationship
with another woman. This woman used to find excuses to be
near me; also she happened to be very attractive. The affair
carried on for about six months. It was not exactly something
I enjoyed and I always felt utterly disgusted with myself. It
all ended when, in a moment of remorse, she upped and spilt
the whole sordid tale to her husband. This poor bloke was
handicapped by having a very weak constitution and I suppose he must have realised that his wife, who went by the
real old-fashioned name of Rosie, had a sexual appetite that
he was unable to satisfy. Once Rosie had enjoyed a couple of
rounds with me I couldn't get shot of her. He came knocking
on the door one evening at Portpool Lane and that was it.
Freda learned about my misdeeds; also the fact that the poor
bloke was shouting his head off made certain that the whole
of Nigel Buildings learned about them, too. I finally managed to calm the lad by convincing him that I had no idea
that Rosie was a married woman. The blows that he was

trying to rain on me were like chaff in the wind, and there was no way I could bring myself to land one on him. In the end he staggered off and I shut the front door and braced myself for the going over I expected to get. Freda had been silent through all the noise and after the lad left she remained silent. I made a couple of cups of tea which she accepted without comment, and after about an hour she finally took hold of my hands and gave me a lecture on the subject of women.

'I am quite aware of how easy it is to trap a man,' she went on. 'I know that deep down you really do love me and the kids and I was also impressed by the way you treated that poor man. I expected you to give him a thumping, but you chose not to and that's to your credit. As far as I'm concerned, Vic, it's in the past, but please don't let me down ever again.'

After that we went on living together as if nothing had happened. But now, many years later, I realise that although Freda had tried to put it behind her it must have rankled and the way I had been living my life had finally stretched her to the limit.

I'd always thought along the lines that somehow or other the two of us would eventually settle down as we got older and the kids went their different ways, but as always Freda had looked at it from a much more practical point of view. Freda was no dreamer. She saw everything in black and white, yes or no, no ifs or buts, spit it out, don't wander or dither. I knew that she was only being realistic about the way we lived together, both of us as obstinate as the day was long, both of us striving for something better, neither of us finding it easy to give ground.

12

How Did I Get Myself in this Predicament?

I barely saw Freda over the next few weeks. Every day she left home for the hostel in Wandsworth and if she came home early it was only to check on Judith. With the two boys now married and living their own lives, I used to get home and find the instructions for cooking my meal written down on a notepad that Freda kept fixed to the wall. I did make it a rule never to go to bed until Freda was home. I know she noticed all this and thought she was having serious misgivings about what she had said about us parting. But a barrier had grown between us and it just seemed that there was no way around it. As for me, I just went for all the overtime I could get. My hours and Freda's hours hardly overlapped at all and our sleeping arrangements had changed. I slept in one of the boys' old rooms.

'Are you going to be home on Sunday, Vic?' Freda asked me one Friday evening.

'If you want, of course.'

'I was thinking we might go out and have a meal and a drink together, you know, like we used to.'

'I'd like nothing better.'

'That's what we'll do then.' And for the first time for weeks we sat down together and watched some idiotic soap on our new telly.

The following Sunday Judith and I went to Brighton on my ageing Triumph 650cc Thunderbird, with Judith on the back clutching all her bathing kit. We hit the A23 with not a care in the world. Knocking along at a steady sixty, I got to thinking that there was no way Freda could be serious about divorce. Later the two of us sat on the pebbles on the beach at Brighton. Judith was trying to do two operations in one, drying her hair and trying to dress herself while covered with the big bath towel she had brought along.

'Are you and Mum getting along a bit better these days? You haven't had a good fight for at least a fortnight. You wouldn't ever leave home, would you, Dad?'

'No Judith, I'd never leave you and Mum. Matter of fact we're going out tonight to have a meal and a drink. Your mum's got it all planned. Anyway, what made you ask a silly question like that?'

'Give over, Dad, the walls in our place are paper-thin. I heard what you and Mum were talking about the other night, it made me cry. Now you tell me it ain't true?'

I looked at my daughter and for the first time I didn't see a child. Judith was now fourteen, going on fifteen. She remind me of Peggy, my very first love who was always chiding me about the future I should be planning for. Now here's my daughter telling me in her own words that her mum and dad are in trouble and she thinks she might lose one of them. She might lose her dad who she has always looked to as protection against any threats. It's true it was her mother who sorted out her troubles, but as with most young girls it's her dad she hero-worships. I said to her, 'Years and years ago, when I was much younger than you are now, Judith, my dad said something to me that I have never forgotten. He said to me, "Whatever happens, son, always love your mother, never let her down, she's always in the right." That's all I can say to you now, whatever comes about, your mum's in the right and, whatever happens, both of us will always love you. Come on, get dried off, we'll 'ave a nice cuppa tea and make our way home, can't be late for the dinner tonight. Your mum says she's paying.'

But despite all my assurances my daughter's eyes were full of tears. I could sense her unhappiness and I cursed myself. Never did it occur to me to place any of the blame on Freda. I was well aware of my failings. I knew that whatever excuses I made I was the one who was still firing away, keeping the trigger depressed and causing murder and mayhem to anyone who dared to confront me. I may have quietened down on the outside but the cancer that had sprouted from the violence I had been witness to was still there. I had never at any time since the end of the war spoken about those five days in Dresden. To all and sundry my war had been like a Cook's tour, and if I had told anyone, who would listen? No: far better to keep these things to myself.

I had to hope that in time the nightmares that plagued me would go away and I would be left in peace. These dark moments in my life, whether they occur in broad daylight or in the middle of the night, always follow the same pattern. I am positioned in a long, semi-dark tunnel. I'm not aware of any ground level or ceiling height. I'm aware of being trapped, I know that I am about to be attacked, but however much I try to move, to get away, there is a force that's holding me down, a heavy weight pressing down on me. I try to run, but my limbs refuse to move. The only part of the dream that changes is the tunnel; at times it seems to close in on me, and at other times the walls seem far apart and everything is much larger. The common factor in these dreams is the attempt to free myself, and I always fail. Sometimes I am searching for Freda and the kids but I can never find them. Only the return to consciousness brings relief.

How long these dreams go on for I haven't a clue; it is said that a dream passes through the brain in a flash, but I have experienced variations of the dream while I have apparently been wide awake in the middle of the day. Luckily, as the years go by these dark moments are slowly vanishing. This is the first time I have ever mentioned them or tried to put them down in writing. I am not making excuses for the way I have behaved. Other men have suffered the same as I did and some of them have made a go of life and succeeded.

We got home to find that Freda had gone to work earlier in the day. She left directions to the restaurant and instructions that I was to be there by seven sharp, when she had a table booked. Getting dressed up for a Sunday night out was a ritual that had passed me by for the last ten years. Judith was looking at me and said that she didn't know that I was so handsome. 'Your mum's treating me to a night out, you be good and don't stop up too late. I haven't a clue what we're up to when we've finished this meal, Mum's got everything planned', and with that I give my daughter a peck on the cheek and I'm on my way to the bus stop.

The restaurant turned out to be one of those French/ Italian jobs that were springing up everywhere. The menu was written in French, there were a couple of Greek waiters thrown in for good measure, and a selection of potted plants to convince the clientele that this was the genuine article. Goodbye fish and chips; instead the chips would be served with some Belgian horsemeat doped up with various small pieces of vegetable and spiced up with garlic. So long as the meat course had the word 'boeuf' in it or something of that nature the punters would pay the earth. I arrived five minutes early but Freda had beaten me to it. 'Come on then, Vic, let's go in and have a nice meal.'

I get another kick in the guts when this lad from somewhere well south of Dover comes up and greets Freda: 'Good evening, Freda, we haven't seen you for a couple of weeks.'

I just sat and said nothing. Freda hadn't expected this from the waiter, but she responded as if it was nothing out of the ordinary. 'Well, what do you expect me to do while you're gallivanting all over the country night after night? And if you're thinking that I've been coming here or any other place with some fancy man you'd be wrong again. I've got a bunch of friends, all women, and we occasionally have a night on the town. They're all in the same boat as me, married but without a husband. Now pay attention to the menu and order what takes your fancy. I don't mind if you order some of that muck you call beer, I'm having a glass of Chardonnay.'

'What's that then?'

'Vic, order your choice and try to grow up.'

When we had eaten our supper I said to Freda, 'I take back everything I said, love. I enjoyed that meal. Now, tell me the real reason why we're sitting here.'

It became obvious to me that Freda was having trouble. She turned her head away and I thought that she was wiping away the start of a tear.

'I've asked you to come here, Vic, because I know you'll never do anything to show me up. If I started talking about what I'm going to say now and we were indoors you would blow your top and we'd finish up having another slanging match.' And then she came out with it. I could sense the difficulty she was having trying to start saying what was on her mind. I reach out and clasped her hand.

'Get it off your chest, love, I won't make a scene.'

'Vic, don't get all lovey-dovey with me now, if I start crying I'm lost. I've been to see a solicitor about a divorce, and what's more you've got to play your part and help me.'

I'd only supped up half of the pint of bitter that stood on the table in front of me; just as well I was still in command of my senses.

'Hold on, love, you can't be serious. You want me to help you end our life together? Who have you been talking to, giving you these ideas? I tell you what, let's not waste the evening. Let's go up to Hammersmith, there's a good film on at the Odeon.'

'No, Vic, I want it all sorted tonight, right here. Vic, we've been together for the past twenty-two years. I know you better than you know yourself. It's not that I shall ever lose my affection for you but that's not enough for me, Vic. I've got a chance to make something of myself now. I can justify my life, I can help these young girls have a decent life, but I need my freedom more than living in hope that all of a sudden you will see the light and take me in your arms again.' Freda paused. 'Something happened to you, Vic, and I don't know what it was. You've never said anything to explain why you're so uptight all the time. I can't remember the last time I heard you laugh. You have to understand, Vic, I'm all broken up. I don't need you as a wage-earner, I need you as a husband and a lover. If you really love me as you say, then tell me when have you ever shown it? Sometimes it's been like heaven, but then you go into these moods, you get another job and we don't see you for weeks, except when you come home and plonk down a fortune in wages. You've never seemed to understand, Vic, money is bread and butter, what we can't do without, but there's more to life than money on the table, the kids have grown up with only half a father. You need a fresh start, Vic, a new struggle you can get your teeth into without having to worry about anything else.' After that long passage of words she paused and took a sip of the wine that as yet she had hardly tasted.

'You have to go down to Brighton, Vic. I've got it all written down here in this envelope. It will give you the name of the hotel; there will be a man and a woman there to meet you. You have to go up to a room, put a dressing gown on, the woman will get into the bed and then this chap will enter the room and take a photo of the two of you. You don't have to get into bed with her, the important thing will be the photo. After that I go to a magistrates' court and sue for divorce on the grounds of infidelity. You don't even have to turn up; all we have to do is to sign a document making it legal for you to pay me a weekly or monthly sum for Judith's upbringing. There, now, I've said what I brought you here for. It hasn't been easy for me to take these steps, Vic. It don't mean that we can't be friends and of course you can always see Judith whenever you want.' She sat back as if preparing herself for an onslaught that she thought was certain to erupt, but it didn't. It was as if I had been hit with a sledge-hammer. I tried to come up with an answer, but my mind was a blank. Finally, as far as I remember I came up with something like this.

'I'll tell you what, Freda. I will agree to your wishes because I know that you're justified in talking to me like this. I'm quite aware that I have not been a good father or husband, but I did think that I was at last getting on the right track. I like this job on the buses, it might well be just another menial job with little or no prospects, but at least I'm trying. I'll do what you say on the condition that you don't get involved with another man for at least six months. If we can last those six months free of each other then I will let you go. In the meantime I will look around for some place to live and promise not to annoy you. I can't believe that we could ever be divorced.' I remember asking her if she had said anything to the boys but she told me that so far it was only between the two of us.

'If I move out first without waiting for the divorce, if it ever comes to that, which I can't for the life of me ever imagine, then the children will know it's all my fault, which I know is the truth. If nothing else, I want them to continue to love their mother in the way they've been brought up. Next week I will have a look around for a decent room. Perhaps then if you have doubts you can always pop around and we can chat each other up. I just can't get my head round what's happening, Freda, but I really do understand that I have a whole lot to answer for. It's just that I thought that at last I was on the right track.'

I left anything else unsaid and of all the nights in my life, with everything I have lived through, that night with Freda in that little restaurant off Putney High Street stands out in my memory like no other. There was one other time when I felt the ground moving under my feet, way back through the years when that German officer all dressed up in his immaculate black uniform with its silver buttons and braid had told my mate Harry and me that we were to be taken away to a place of execution. That was before the Dresden episode, and it was one of the few moments in my life that I really thought all was lost.

The result of this evening meant that I was a sort of out-cast in a world I still didn't really understand. Freda had been right when she said, 'We always felt safe with you, Vic,

I know that you don't get scared easily, but you are scared of going out in the world on your own. You've never bothered or tried to understand the other person's point of view. The majority of people like this lot in here are not like us. They don't want to get involved with anything controversial, they are very happy just going to work to earn money, going home to the wife and kids and enjoying a quiet evening watching the telly. They read the *Daily Mirror*, the *Sun* and the *Daily Mail* and they vote for whoever looks the best in a photo, but you can never bring yourself to even try to understand that all they want is a peaceful life.'

Then she carried on, driving the knife in ever deeper.

'We've both chosen in our life to fight what we consider is evil. The difference between us, Vic, is that I have made it a point to see things from other viewpoints. You never have. Not only that, you have this terrible tendency to tear into people whose ideas you don't agree with. You're not frightened of anything physical, Vic, you're scared of what you don't understand.'

Outside the restaurant I waited while she retrieved her coat. I helped her on with it and said: 'I suppose we can walk home together, then?'

'I have to be up early in the morning, Vic, let's call a cab.'

'No, you go on your own love, I want to walk it.'

'To tell you the truth, Vic, if I walk home with you it will finish me. I'll never be able to go through with what I've talked about. Despite everything, Vic, I know in my heart, whatever I tell other people, I will always love you.' Then she waved down a passing cab and was whisked away, leaving me on the kerbside in Putney High Street, not knowing whether I was coming or going. My old Rifle Brigade mate Terry, who had introduced me to the Dawson brothers, had hit the nail on the head when he said, 'We're all fucked up, Vic, the lot of us.' It occurred to me as I was left standing outside that restaurant that Terry must have loved his wife a bundle, but she had had enough after the first twelve months. I wondered if Terry was right; was there no chance for the likes of us? Were we indeed 'all fucked up'?

Walking home along the Upper Richmond Road I was so bombed out of my mind that I did not realise a police car had pulled up beside me. 'You OK, matey, ain't 'ad one too many, have you?' I must have satisfied their curiosity. 'Go steady then, mate', and with a cheery wave they were on their way. By the time I got home the flat was in darkness. I climbed the short flight of stairs thinking, 'How am I going to give all this up?' And my face was wet with tears that I couldn't hold back.

By midweek I had found a room off Putney High Street, quite close to the bus depot. I had a single ground-floor room that looked out on to the backyard. It was furnished with a bed, a couple of sorry looking and well-used armchairs and a small cooker that had to be plugged into a multi-point socket that used to get red hot and switch itself off. It was going to cost me £5 a week and the house was run and owned by an ageing Jewish lady who had another three rooms let out, all to men. When I took the room she made the point that she didn't look kindly on any of her men 'bringing women or girls into the house. I run a nice house for gentlemen only.' It may not have been the Ritz but it had a comfortable feel about it.

I went through the following weeks in a dream, once again doing all the overtime I could get hold of; anything was better than sitting in that tiny living room-cum-bedroom. I was utterly in despair. I tried to pluck up the courage to go back to what I still considered my home and talk it out with Freda, but to me that was akin to a weakness to which I would never submit. Paying Freda a fiver a week for Judith and then having to fork out another fiver for the rent meant that, given the wages on the buses, my eating arrangements were somewhat irregular. Not only that, I discovered that keeping clothes clean and tidy meant extra expense. In the first month, what with all the overtime I was doing, I lost a stone in weight. The highlight was when I had a few hours with Judith. I would take her out for a meal in a decent restaurant and then to a film or whatever. Taking my daughter out like this meant that cash-wise I would be completely broke for the following week, but it was those little outings that brought light to the drab existence I was now experiencing. Judith used to tell me that her mum was hardly ever home, as her life was almost completely taken over with the routine at the hostel she was now in charge of. She once told me that if Mum kept on like she was doing she would be running the council in next to no time.

True to my word I used to post the money order off every week and kept away from Roehampton. I managed to get a second job with a bank as a security guard. I got this little number via one of the bus drivers who had retired from professional boxing and had been offered this post by his bank manager. It entailed getting to the bank at six in the morning, opening up the side door to let the cleaning ladies in, all four of them, and then locking up after they had finished, which would be around 7 a.m. It was an hour's work five mornings a week, for which he collected a tenner. Being a bus driver meant that one week he would be on a late shift to be followed by an early shift, so he asked me whether I would be interested in doing the alternate week's work. I jumped at it.

Suddenly I had an extra tenner to play with every other week, and that's how my life carried on for the next six months. I once asked Judith how her two brothers were getting along. 'Oh, them two, we hardly ever see them, perhaps once a fortnight one of them might come around. I think they are OK, but really, Dad, I don't know.'

What little hope I was still nursing in my mind that the nightmare might come to a natural end sunk a few more fathoms when I received notification that I would be expected to turn up at this hotel in Brighton to supply the evidence for the divorce. 'I hope you're not going to get up on your hind legs over this, Vic, just let me have it my way this once.' I didn't answer the letter but I made the effort and delivered myself to the three people at the address in Brighton. One of them wore a business suit complete with blue tie. I presumed he must be the solicitor's clerk; the other lad had a Rolleiflex camera with a flash. The woman kept in the background although her attitude, the manner in which she carried herself, suggested to me that of the three she was the one who really understood the nature of what was about to happen. I got the feeling she had done this a lot.

I had to check in with my name and address; once that was done the girl at the reception desk showed us to a room and disappeared. I had to pay for the room but I had been warned about this and luckily had the cash. The chap in the suit claimed the receipt.

So I'm in this bedroom alone with this woman. 'It will all be over in a matter of seconds,' she tells me, 'no need for you to get undressed, that is unless you want a bit of love. You've paid for it, you know.' I could feel the disgust growing inside me. The woman must have been aware of my feelings. 'C'mon, ducks, put that dressing gown on. I slip into this bed and then you give the door a tap.' I followed the instruction, in popped the photographer, the room burst into light as he popped his flash, and in no time the woman is dressed and facing me. 'I know what you're going through, believe me I do, and now it's all done with. If you want to you can buy me a nice cup of tea on the way to the station. C'mon, ducks.' And she pilots me out of the door and the next thing I know is that the two of us are sitting in this little café just around the corner. By now she has prised my name out of me. 'Look at it this way, Victor, with a bit of luck the sun will be shining tomorrow, by then you will be on the way to getting over it, it's not the end of the world, you know.' I never did have a name for this woman but on that day she helped me as she had probably helped other men in a similar predicament.

13

The Divorce

After about two months I received a large brown envelope addressed to Mr Victor James Gregg, informing me that a judgement would be delivered against me on a charge of infidelity brought to the court by Mrs Freda Gregg, at the following time and date. The hearing was to be held at the Westminster Magistrates' Court in the Strand, London. The following day I had a letter from Freda telling me that it would not be necessary for me to attend the hearing as the evidence against me was cut and dried. Giving up without a fight was not part of my character, although I was still finding it difficult to believe that this was happening. If I turned up and could really explain to Freda how much she meant to me and how I would miss the children there was no way that she would be able to go through with the end of our marriage. So poor was my understanding of my handling of the marriage that I never even recognised that suddenly speaking or thinking about 'the children' only showed just how little I had involved myself with our family life. The boys were no longer children – they were grown up and married – and if I had managed to get near enough on that fateful morning to put that plea to Freda she would have made verbal mincemeat of me.

I turned up at the court but was refused permission to approach the benches. I called out to Freda who, unlike me, was sitting on a posh seat at the front of the Court, with her big overweight solicitor on one side and the man from Brighton on the other. I had hardly opened my mouth to voice my cry of protest when I was immediately accosted by two policemen and moved back to the rear of the courtroom. The magistrate, or whoever he might be, was pronouncing judgement as I was being bundled out of the main entrance. One of the coppers said to me, 'Keep calm, mate, you ain't doing yourself a service by carrying on like this.'

Freda eventually came out, slipped her arm into mine and led me across the road to a small restaurant near the courthouse. We sat opposite each other and she took my hand in hers. 'It's done now, Vic. You know, it might be true what you said. Maybe we can't live without each other. Who knows what the future holds? We might get married again, but surely you realise, Vic, we were getting nowhere living the way we were?' Freda caught a bus back to work while I roamed the backstreets of Covent Garden going back through the years. I was totally lost. I went back to my digs in Putney to wallow in self-pity.

Freda knew where I was living but kept her distance; we were so near and yet so far from each other. At the end of the first six months I was at the crossroads. I was scared of asking her to meet me because I wasn't sure how I might react if she refused. Could I stand an outright rejection? Freda herself once again stepped in where I was faltering. She was waiting for me by the bus stop in Putney High Street as I finished my shift, having sussed out my timetable. It was three o'clock in the afternoon. I noticed that the conductress who had been working with me followed the two of us as we made our way into the main high street. Freda suggested that we have 'a nice cuppa tea in the Express Dairy tea shop down by the bridge'. I just wanted to grab her and never let her go but had the sense to realise that this was not going to happen.

'I want to thank you, Vic, for keeping your word about not annoying me, and for the way you have kept the payments up, and I know that you have been sending some extra to Judith.'

She then went on about how I was managing.

'Have you found anyone you like yet? Who was that conductress that you had with you?'

I told her that I was doing two jobs now and all the overtime I could get. What time I had to myself I just went to the room and crashed out.

'You haven't even had a night out with anyone in all these sixth months?'

''fraid not, love. To tell the truth, I don't think I could stomach another woman now. I wouldn't wish to go through this again.' I was getting my own back with a vengeance. Even before I had finished that little outburst I was aware of the mental pain that Freda might be going through. I apologised.

'I'm sorry, Freda, I have the sense to know that you've nothing to blame yourself for. I've had plenty of time to think about our life and I know it's all my fault. Don't worry about me, you know I can survive. It's just going to take time. All I ask is that you keep in touch, even if it's only at Christmas.' I went up to the counter, paid and walked away.

This time at least I was the one who walked away first. I left my Freda sitting alone in this Express Dairy tea room. I consoled myself with the thought that at least she had Judith for company, along with the flat in Roehampton, and, even more importantly, she had a bright future ahead of her. I walked down to the riverside and along past the boathouses.

I toyed with the idea of getting boozed up, but I couldn't even stomach that. I finally arrived back at my pokey little room. I took my shoes off, lay on the bed and collapsed into the land of nod. That is until around about ten in the evening when I awoke and finished up in the local fish and chip shop.

The week following that meeting with Freda was one of memories that I couldn't put away. I must have been like a robot, turning up for work, sitting on my own in the garage canteen, not aware that the day was passing. To be followed by the next day and the next.

The conductress who I was working with on that week's shift was a nice looking woman. The striking thing about her was her head of red hair. I wondered if she had a temper to go with it. As soon as we arrived at a terminus she jumped out to get the tea from whatever hole-in-the-wall café was nearby.

'Was that your girlfriend who you met last week then, Vic? She seemed a nice person.'

'She's my ex-wife, we got a divorce six months ago, and I'd rather not talk any more about it, Bett. I don't want to be rude, but that's it.'

I upped and left the table and deposited myself back in the bus waiting for Bett's tinkle on the bell to tell me that we're on our way again. This Bett had another habit that I noticed: she seldom mixed with the other men and women in the canteen but I could always find her tucked away in some corner immersed in a book. The following morning as we were signing on for the day's shift I said how sorry I was for being so abrupt. 'In fact I realised that I had been very rude and I want to say sorry if I offended you.' 'I was never offended, Vic, in fact I felt a touch sorry for you. You got any kids?' I told her about the situation and repeated that I didn't want to talk about it. She never mentioned the subject again, much to my relief. I didn't want the whole garage to know what a failure I had been.

It was some three weeks later, about four in the afternoon, and I was attempting to iron a shirt and a pair of trousers when Mrs Jacobs, who we all called Elsie, knocked on my door to tell me that a nice young lady wished to see me. 'She can come in, Victor, but remember, no argy bargy.' I'm feeling good because I have an unknown visitor. 'Thanks, Mrs Jacobs, that's kind of you. The 'nice young lady' was Bett, all dressed up in a summer frock, her hair all nicely curled. She was a sight for sore eyes, as the saying goes. I invited her in. Luckily I had dusted and cleaned the room up the day before. 'I can see you keep it nice and clean. Sit down, Vic, and I'll make a cup of tea and I'll put an iron to this shirt you're ruining.'

Bett got straight to the point. 'Seeing we're both off tonight I thought you might like to take me to the pictures up at Hammersmith.' With that she made the pot of tea she had mentioned and finished ironing my shirt. As we drank the tea she suddenly said, 'I'm in the same boat as you, Vic, all on my lonesome. It can't be right for the two of us single people not to have a night out now and again.' She carried on about where she lived and that she'd been thinking about how nice it might be if I were to ask her out one evening but seeing that the invitation was not forthcoming she had decided to 'test the water', so to speak. I was almost at the point of turning her down, but it had been years since anyone had been interested enough in me to want to spend an evening with me. Yes, I decided, it was a nice thought and, yes, I would be delighted to take her out for the evening.

With that she left the room with instructions where to pick her up at any time after six thirty. 'Don't forget, Vic, if we're going to Hammersmith we got to allow for the bus being late.'

I returned to my room to find Elsie in the passageway.

'She looks a nice young lady, Victor, better than sitting on your own if you ask me.'

'Mrs Jacobs, would you mind if I called you Elsie?'

The lady of the house looked at me and paused, and there was a silence between us. I continued.

'A long time ago, in my youth, a Jewish lady of a similar age to yourself gave me a job when I was out of work. She turned out to be a sort of fairy godmother to me and she ended up treating me as if I was her only child. She was called Maisie and she never had any children of her own. She used to say to me, "Victor, don't call me Missus or anything like that, my name is Maisie." You know what, Mrs Jacobs, next to my mother and my wife, or, rather, ex-wife, she's the only woman who's ever meant anything to me.'

Elsie broke in, saying, 'You've been here eight months now, Victor, you know that every one of you men calls me Elsie, and to me that tells me that you respect me. That means a lot to a lonely old Jewish widow. I tell you what, Victor, if you want someone to talk to, come downstairs and we'll have a cup of tea together, and I've just finished baking a fruit cake'. With that she started off to the staircase leading to her base-ment flat. I followed her down the narrow stairs, taking note of her advice to be careful of the bottom step. After telling me to make myself comfortable Elsie disappeared into her small kitchen. Her tiny abode was furnished in the typical old Jewish style complete with heavy velvet curtains and golden threaded cords to close them. Photographs in heavy ornate silver frames, pictures of elderly ladies and their husbands of ages gone past. Nothing seemed out of place. Elsie was Elsie and this was her home. One fitted the other. When she had put the tea on the table she went to a cupboard and brought out a half-section of fruit cake and a couple of small tea plates. She poured out the tea and looked at me.

'Now, if you want to, Victor, you can get it all off your chest, and don't worry too much, I've been taking in young men like yourself for the past thirty odd years, you're not the first whose needed to tell me stuff.'

'The nice young lady has asked me to spend the evening with her. I've accepted her invitation but I'm not happy about it, not one bit.' Elsie was looking at me but didn't interrupt, so I charged on. 'Part of me wants her company but the other half warns about the harm I can do if I let her down, that is if she gets too much attached to me. Elsie, you remind me of Maisie. She would have explained things to me. It's true that I'm not sixteen any more. I've seen the back of forty but I know that Maisie would have sorted me out.' I carried on in fits and starts. It must have taken me nearly half an hour to open up my mind to my landlady; baring my soul, with pauses and disjointed sentences, was a new experience for me. I remember thinking that I was talking to Elsie as a child might talk to his or her teacher. Elsie stood silent for a moment.

'That was a mouthful, Victor. Do you realise what you've been talking to me about? And me being almost a stranger.' She paused 'Did you serve in the war, Victor?' I gave her a potted history and ended by telling her what I remembered about my experiences at Dresden.

'Victor, like your Maisie I'm Jewish, but more than that I am German by birth. My parents managed to get me to

England in 1936 for which I shall be ever grateful to this
country. My father was sent to a camp and my mother never
heard from him again. She was killed in an air raid on Cologne
in 1941 and, like you, I suspect neither of us has ever got
over the experience. I'm not going to listen about your mari-
tal problems. I've witnessed the results of similar situations
ever since I started taking men like yourself into my house,
but I will offer you this piece of advice: if you think, or have
confidence, that you have learned the lesson of your failures,
then take the young lady out for the evening. You have to
keep on trying in this world.' She paused again. 'Don't ever
hope that you can make it up with your ex-wife; no woman
of any standing is ever going to consider such a final thing
as a divorce unless she knows in herself that all trust has
gone. Even if the two of you agreed to give it another go,
you would live a life of always being on your guard, it would
never again be the same.' Yet another pause. 'There you are,
Victor, you have my blessing for what it's worth. Now go and
get yourself cleaned up and go and meet your new girlfriend.
You never can tell; she might be what you are looking for.'

And that is what I did. Bit by bit Bett and I became more
confident with each other. We worked together whenever we
could arrange it, but we never allowed things to get out of
hand. I suspected that Bett would have popped into bed with
me in a flash if I had given the slightest of hints but I wasn't
ready for that relationship. Over twenty years with one
woman is not something that can be discarded overnight.
Bett said that she wanted to meet Freda.

'Why?'

'I want to make sure that I'm not breaking up a
marriage.'

'But we're divorced, you know that.'

'Yes, I know, but you still have feelings for each other. Before we go any further, Vic, I want to hear it from Freda. Call it getting her OK about what may become of us.'

'If that's what you want, and I think Freda would like it as well. Perhaps you'll learn a few things about me that will put you off. I'm not the easiest of blokes to live with, if that's what you're thinking of.'

'We've all got our faults and our hidden secrets. Vic, before things go too far with us I'll tell you about my dark past, I promise. In the meantime let's approach the foreman and see if we can go on crewing together, even if we can't live together, which I think I would really like.' And with that promise of possible future bliss, she jumped on a bus that was going up Fulham Palace Road to take her to the room she rented.

I posted off a letter to Freda telling her about Bett's request and a couple of days later I had a note from her saying that she would be more than delighted to meet up with my new girlfriend, 'Even if only to put her mind at rest'. The two of them met at the Robin Hood, a pub at the bottom of Roehampton Lane, and they got on like a house on fire. I learned later that Freda had given Bett her blessing and wished her well. 'There's nothing really bad about him, he's over forty and still thinks he's in his teens, and what's more if you don't put your foot down he'll work twenty-four hours a day and you'll end up a right grass widow. You have to stand up to him, Bett, keep him on track. If he starts going on long walks of an evening it's not because he's seeing some chick, it's a forewarning that he's becoming bored. The next thing you know he's got another job that's going to turn the pair of you into millionaires.'

Freda told Bett about the time I almost killed her brother-in-law, all because of an innocent remark, adding that she didn't think I was completely normal even after all this time. 'It's something to do with what happened the second time he went to war; when he finally came back he was a changed man. There's one good thing about him, he'll never lay a hand on you.' Freda told Bett that if I ever went for somebody just get between the pair of us and to tell me to calm down. 'By the next morning he won't remember anything about it. I think the war did something to him, Bett, but he's never let on to anyone about anything. If you ask me, he's still searching for peace, it just might be that he's found it in you.' Bett told me that Freda had praised her for her courage and decency coming forward like she had. Apparently Freda had said, 'I wish from my heart that Vic finds his peace with you, Bett. We both tried our hardest but it never did work out.'

Bett had been a clippie for seventeen years. What she didn't know about handling people in awkward situations wasn't worth knowing. She had a way about her that put everyone at peace. Without seemingly doing anything she could calm a whole bus load of passengers. There were many times when she showed her skill, like when we were working the No. 16s out of Cricklewood to Victoria on a late shift coming up through Edgware Road passing all the Irish pubs; or on the 14s doing Putney to Hornsey Rise through the West End, when maybe Scotland had lost to the Sassenachs at a footer game at Wembley. The lads from Glasgow and beyond would stagger on to the bus en route for King's Cross and the train ride home. I remember one occasion when at half ten at night we picked up a bunch of lads at Piccadilly. The bus had only gone as far as the Hippodrome – five hundred yards, give or take – and I feel the bus shaking. Bett gave a triple ring on the bell and

I anchored up and nipped round to see what the trouble was. I found her quietly escorting these two Jocks off the bus and on to the pavement while the two protagonists are still hammering away at each other. Having succeeded with no assistance from any of the fear-stricken passengers, or rabbits as we used to call them, she said, 'All done, Vic, let's go.' That's my Bett: as calm as a whisper of a breeze in midsummer. Not so with the well-doused Irish lads at the other end of Oxford Street. Anywhere between Marble Arch and Kilburn we were liable to be inundated by a bunch of them who, when well into their cups, never raised a fist in anger. Instead they would invariably burst into some sentimental song about the beauty and glory of the Emerald Isle.

Bett told me that Freda had said that after the divorce had gone through it was like going on holiday. All of a sudden she was free to do her own thing. She also told Bett that if I had insisted we walk home together after that night in the restaurant in Putney it was possible she would have crumbled and called it all off. Bett undertook to make certain that my payments to Judith were kept up and that was that. My future was all but wrapped up, without my knowing, naturally.

Bett and I eventually found a small flat and that's where I discovered that there really was a Sea of Tranquillity. From that day onward my life took a different tack. I put Bett on a number one priority list. I was determined never to make the same mistakes that had ruined Freda's life. I probably owe all the happiness I've enjoyed in this second life to Freda's down-to-earth view of the situation. One thing I know for a fact: the love that bound us together in those years of war and terror never left us. Deep down we knew that we had lost something that was beautiful. We kept in constant touch with each other as we both went our different ways and enjoyed very different lives. As for me, I was on the path of a new life, and I vowed that this time I wouldn't mess it all up. At last, I was living in a world with no friction and no stress. I must be doing the right things at last.

14

The Sea of Tranquillity

After we had been living together for a year I asked Bett if she would consider getting married to me and without any hesitation she said yes. It seemed that my dark days had finally come to an end.

After the wedding we managed to wheedle a fortnight's leave from the job. I had bought an ageing Ford Eight. We stuffed a change of clothing into a battered old suitcase that Bett said was part of her dark past and off we went. We had no destination; we just stopped at any pub that advertised bed and breakfast. In Taunton we discovered that the local bus company were so hard up for crews that the council would provide us with housing if we signed on with the company. And so we cut the ties with London and moved away from the city, never to return. We were both starting a new life. We got our job with the Western Bus Company and the council gave us a lovely ground-floor flat complete with a large garden. I became aware that my feelings for Bett had changed. She was becoming part of me, we were turning into a unit, and the hurt of the divorce died down.

Getting the job on the local bus service served its purpose in so far as it provided us with this nice living accommodation but eventually I rebelled against the boring monotony of the job and set myself up in business as an industrial decorator, and things turned out well.

Being my own boss enabled me to set a living schedule that suited my moods. Bett, bearing in mind Freda's warnings, suggested that it might be good for me to get away on my own for a couple of weeks. This would suit her down to the ground as it enabled her to get up to Edinburgh and visit her mum and sisters. She could read me like a book and knew that visiting the in-laws was not my sort of thing. I didn't need a second invitation. I bought myself a brand new BMW R80 motorcycle, and sometime around 1972 I had a trip to Sweden set up as part of a British contingent to a town called Jönköping, where a large international motorcycling rally, or Treff, was being held.

I decided to travel via the DDR, better known as East Germany, the part that was controlled by those nasty Russians! I arranged the tourist visa with my old friends at Berolina Travel, in Conduit Street. A couple of the older hands remembered me and I was given the visa without the usual formalities. The general idea was that on the return trip I would proceed through the DDR, spend a couple of days in Dresden, perhaps lay a wreath if I could get one, carry on to Prague and then home.

15

I'm At It Again

When the Swedish rally finished I made my way south via the sea crossing to Sesnitz, a port on the northern coast of the German Democratic Republic. I had an uneventful trip down from the north, bypassing Berlin and arrived in the middle of the Harz Forest looking for a campsite. I followed signs for *Campingplatz, 2 km* and found myself by a lake, where, instead of tents, there was a collection of huts.

By now it was quite late in the evening. No sooner had I stopped than I was surrounded by a crowd of people all standing and gawping at my brand new BMW. At first I took no notice of them and unloaded my gear. It was then that the first tentative steps were taken by the onlookers to establish my identity. I could hear the mutterings of '*Engländer, Engländer*'. They all continued to look at me as if I was a visitor from outer space. Next I was approached by a young lady who explained to me in English that she was the local schoolteacher and that I had arrived not at a general campsite but at a holiday site for German workers. She quickly added that this was no problem and asked if I wanted to sit down at the communal table and join in the evening meal. I readily accepted the offer. She told me not to bother about the tent and my gear as the older boys and girls would fix everything up for me. I learned that the teacher was called Giselda and told her that my name was Victor. Giselda stuck with me all through the evening, translating the questions and the answers. She said I was the first Englishman some of them had ever met.

She told me that these holiday camps were everywhere in the DDR and that they provided very cheap holidays for factory workers. There was nothing fancy about the arrangements. The toilets (I prefer to call them latrines) consisted of two long sheds, one for either sex. Each hut had a row of wooden seats over a hole in the ground. The system was flushed every hour with water from a huge tank attached high on a tower. There was a row of shovels hanging on the wall next to a heap of soil and it was the responsibility of the campers to fill in the hole at the end of their stay and then dig a new one for those who would take over when they left. Nobody seemed to mind these primitive arrangements, and, as for me, it was nothing compared to the POW camps I had been in. There must have been about eighty families living on the site all having a good time. I was made very welcome and spent a very noisy night with everyone.

It was nearly dawn when I staggered off to the seclusion of my tent, only to be rudely awoken by the sound of giggling children as soon as the sun came up. There were no adults to be seen anywhere. I presumed they were still sleeping off the previous night's party. I put on a brave face and smiled and nodded my head at the incomprehensible language the kids were speaking.

Next I swam out to a raft in the middle of the lake and spent the rest of the morning in heavenly solitude. Back at the tent I decided to do a bit of clothes washing which caused great consternation among the women. It seemed that in the DDR men never did the washing, and my clothing was taken away. When I finally got it back everything was washed far cleaner than I could have managed, and all neatly ironed for good measure. I spent four days on the campsite and on the last evening, everyone started giving me their names and addresses. Suddenly a couple mentioned the name Jünger.

The name seemed familiar, it rang a bell, but I couldn't place it. I went to bed that evening with the name still bothering me – Jünger. I awoke in the middle of the night in a cold sweat. It had clicked: I had met a man called Jünger just after the Battle of Arnhem. He was an old silver-haired German officer with a gammy leg. Surely this could not be the same man. I remembered how he had boasted about his Saxon ancestry.

Next morning I found the couple; the mother was in her hut with her two girls. Marcus, her husband, had gone to the village with the men to get supplies, presumably more beer and schnapps. When he came back we sat around the table in the hut. I asked them to find the young schoolteacher to translate. Then I asked if they knew an Albert Jünger. Silence, then I told them the story of my short association with Silverhair. Marcus said, yes, he did have an Uncle Albert, and, yes, he had been an officer and, yes, he still had all of his hair although sadly no longer silver but white. He added that they were going home in four days and if I came to their flat in Schneefeld I could meet Herr Jünger. Sadly I was on my way home and had to be in Prague by the end of the week. I said I would write as soon as possible. I made a friend of Marcus and his family and visited them whenever I was in the east, but even so several years were to pass before I finally met up with Uncle Albert.

16

Trouble in Two Forms

About three months after I got back I was working at Hinkley Point, the huge nuclear power station in north Somerset, coating up two huge metal containers with two-pack epoxy resin. It hadn't been a good day. I had earned something like £300 for the work but it had left me knackered.

As I was leaving, the security police on the gate told me that there were a couple of gents who wanted to talk to me. Inland Revenue, I thought, and got ready to drive off. 'I wouldn't do that, Vic,' said one of the security lads, 'they look like the law to me'.

He was nearly right, although the two 'well-dressed gentlemen were from the British Intelligence, not the police. When I met them at the gate, the taller of the two spoke up.

'Mr Victor Gregg?'

'That's me.'

'A couple of miles down the road there's a pub.'

'The Cottage,' I answered.

'We noticed it as we came in,' said the shorter of the two. 'I would like to suggest that the three of us have a quick drink and a few words.'

'What about? Is there some sort of trouble? Are you the law?'

'Nothing like that,' said Shorty. 'We're hoping you might be able to help us.'

'I'll see you there,' I said, jumping aboard the BMW.

Ted the publican greeted me by putting my usual bitter in front of me and saying, 'You're a bit early tonight.'

'Do me a favour, Ted, there's two geysers coming in any minute. If they ask for a beer give it to them out of the swill bin.'

'You got enemies, Vic?'

'Could be.' By the time they arrived at the Cottage I was well into my pint. They both ordered lager, the bottled kind.

Lofty kicked off by producing a wallet with a card. What caused me to blink was the wording at the top – 'Ministry of Information' – along with an official looking crown and the man's photograph.

'Tell us what you've been up to since you left the Moscow Bank.'

'You're joking,' I replied. 'That was more than ten years ago.'

'Not joking,' says Shorty. 'But I will tell you that you're not in trouble.'

I signalled to Ted to bring over another pint.

'Been on the London buses for five years, got myself divorced, moved down here and been working like a dog ever since, and I've kept my nose clean.'

'Good enough,' said the taller one. His companion produced a ring file from his briefcase. The last time somebody had produced a file (at Telekabir in Cairo) it had consisted of no more than about ten pages. The bundle that now lay on the table looked more like a telephone directory. Along with the pages that were held in place by the rings, there were other loose-leaf pages, some roughly stapled together. About half a dozen sheets fell on the floor.

'That's not a dossier on me I hope,' says I.

'This is only a copy of what we're interested in at the moment,' says Shorty. By now I was a bit knocked back. Keep to the truth, Vic, I says to myself. 'Now, tell us about your trip to the DDR last August.'

I told them about the rally in Sweden, about the trip to Dresden, about laying a few flowers by the burnt-out Cathedral and the trip home. I left out the details concerning Marcus and his family. 'That was all there was to it,' I said.

'How did you get your visa?'

Keeping to the facts I replied, 'Through Berolina Travel in Conduit Street.'

A short pause.

'And you had no trouble getting in or out?'

'None whatsoever, easy as falling off a bike.'

'Before we go,' said Shorty, 'are you planning to go over again, perhaps next year?'

'Shouldn't think so, once is enough'.

I left them still supping their lagers. As I started to leave the tall one whose name according to his card was Wallace, remarked that I might be hearing from them again. I drove home deep in thought.

After a shower and dinner Bett remarked that I was a bit quiet.

'Anything wrong, Vic?'

'No, love, got to do my books tonight. I'll disappear into the back room for a couple of hours.'

It wasn't the fact that they knew about the DDR trip that worried me; it was obvious that information was being passed on from Berolina Travel. Another worry was that they knew I was working at the nuclear power plant, and what days I would be on site. My work took me all over the South West and even I didn't know for sure where I would be from one day to the next. It was obvious that I was going to hear from them again, but why? In the end I told myself to stop worrying, take things slowly, it'll all come out in the wash. And so the months slipped by and I kept on slaving.

Then, one Saturday morning, when Bett and I were sitting in our little council house garden enjoying the warmth of the summer sunshine, the phone rang and I went inside to answer it.

'Is that Victor?' The caller, a lady, went on to say how distressing it was but she wanted to talk about Frances, her friend. She went on to explain that Frances had no idea that she was phoning me but she wanted to help Frances and had turned to me because she had heard that I was a friend of the family. I had no idea who she was talking about. I couldn't for the life of me bring to mind anyone named Frances.

The distressed woman went rambling on. Had I heard that Tim had been taken into custody? Tim? Then it clicked – Timbo was a local lad, Somerset-born and bred. He had worked with me off and on for the past couple of years. All the gang accepted Timbo despite his sometimes odd ways that only a couple of us understood. Timbo had been in the Merchant Navy in the war and had survived two sinkings, both in the Atlantic. The second time he survived three days in an open boat before being plucked from certain death by a navy frigate. Despite that horrendous experience he had signed on again as soon as they discharged him from convalescence.

That was Timbo, a man who could stand up and defy the odds against him. Timbo's wife had sued for divorce. As his friends understood it she couldn't stand the dark moods that Timbo kept slipping into. As far as I knew she had no idea about her husband's past. Tim had never mentioned any of it. Only his close friends got to know about the terrible experiences that Tim had suffered, and that information was only gleaned when he had had a pint too many, and bits and pieces of his history came spilling out.

It seemed that Timbo was in the nick for inflicting grievous bodily harm on some bloke who was maltreating his ex-wife, Frances. This lady on the telephone, who gave her name as Mabel, didn't know who to turn to as her friend was so distressed. I told her to ring off and I would see what could be done. I wasn't concerned about the wife; Timbo was the problem.

When I told the lads about it on the Monday morning they were worried. None of us could imagine Timbo causing grievous bodily harm to anyone. The next thing we knew was that Timbo was out on police bail. The lad who was my foreman came from a family of farmers and had worked with horses, so his nickname was Bronco. If a job happened to be outside the boundaries of the town, and grazing for the day was available, it wasn't unusual to see Bronco turning up for work astride a horse. Bronco had the build of a heavyweight wrestler which could be very useful when any degree of force was required. Like any man who knows he can handle himself, Bronco never threatened anyone. He was a good mate to have around. Bronco had known Tim since their schooldays so he decided to go and have chat with him to see what all the fuss was about. The rest of us decided that we would get Timbo on to the job we were doing. I had been handed it as a 'sub' by one of Taunton's big building contractors. It was the complete renovation of this large country house, at least five months' work for what was now six of us, and we were being paid a daily rate by the hour.

Building sub-contractors like me didn't like this sort of arrangement because they could not make much money out of it. In this case I had taken on the job as I was aware that the builder was hard-pressed for good labour, and it was well known that nearly all the good paying jobs in the area finished up on his books. Back-scratching again, keeping Mr Jackson the builder happy, would pay dividends in the future, so day work it was. About twice a week his second-in-command would visit the job, make a few suggestions, just to let us know who was in charge. I would get a cheque at the beginning of every month; the amount would be according to the hours indented for and as long as the money tallied with the amount of work done everyone was happy.

By the next morning, the gang of us were sitting around having our dinner break when Bronco told us about his visit to Timbo the evening before. Timbo had been told about this bloke and how he had put his ex-wife Frances's face in plaster. Timbo had gone berserk and lashed out at the man with a car tyre lever which he had armed himself with before the visit. With Timbo swearing and cursing and the kids crying their little eyes out, some neighbour worried about the noise had got on to the local fuzz who had appeared and promptly cuffed Timbo and charged him.

One of the lads piped up that the only way to save Timbo was to somehow convince this bloke that appearing in court as evidence against our mate would not be a sensible way of acting. Another one of Timbo's mates said that the man had arrived in the area from Birmingham only recently; that told us that he wouldn't have many friends in the locality. The dinner hour went from one hour and into two and it was decided that the only way of saving Timbo from doing a lengthy stretch was to confront the man and convince him that moving back to Brum would be a better option than having the shape of his face altered. Timbo being out on bail could be a problem. Bronco decided that he and I would be sufficient to make this bloke see the error of his ways. One of the other lads said he would keep Timbo away from the scene of battle.

I didn't know much about the lifestyle of these country boys but I had never come across groups that stuck together so closely. All six of this little workforce that I had hired were reared in and around Taunton, and they were probably all related. This meant that anyone who did ill to one of their own did so at his peril. The more I learned about these Somerset people the more I admired them. All this didn't bode well for the man from Birmingham who had slashed the face of this local girl, Timbo's ex-wife.

The following day Bronco came up to me. 'You ready for this, Vic? You know it's none of your business?' I told him we'll have our 'muggo' (dinner break, for the uninitiated) and then we'll go and sort the lad out.

Part of my toolkit, the old brass knuckleduster, had lain dormant since the days at Borehamwood. This was a new life I was leading; violent confrontations were a thing of the past. And yet I fished out this evil piece of weaponry as calmly as if it was an ordinary everyday tool. I slipped it into the pocket of my overalls still wrapped in the same old sock of years ago; not only that but, here I was, well past my forties with my sell-by date fast approaching.

We arrive at Timbo's house, the one he's not allowed into any more, and his ex opens the door, her face a mass of bruises, her bottom lip swollen and covered in some yellowy medication. She greeted the pair of us half-heartedly. Bronco saw the little girl and boy hiding behind the mother, and said to the boy, 'Where's your uncle, then?' The boy pointed up the stairs leading to the bedrooms.

But then, to save us the trouble of going up, down comes the object of our visit. Bronco stood, legs apart, his massive arms folded to bar the way. Meanwhile, I succeeded in edging the mother and the two kids into the kitchen at the far end of the passage. The man made a swing at Bronco who took a step back and tripped over a broom that was lying on the floor. The man was about to kick Bronco in the face when I tapped him on the shoulder and, as he swung around, the big brass knuckleduster landed full square behind his ear. He went down pole-axed. Bronco looked at me, I nodded back. 'No need to worry, he's not dead, we've got at least ten minutes to collect his gear and throw it out on to the road.' Which, with the help of the boy, we proceeded to do. The mother just sat there speechless. As we were finishing chucking the last of the man's belongings out into the street he started to come round. Bronco stood above him, and I said, 'We don't look with much favour around here on men who beat their women. Move away, mate, that's your only chance of survival.'

Bronco then squared up to the mother. 'You threw away a bloody good mate of ours. We didn't do this for you, just for Timbo.' With that we waved to the two kids and went about our business. The man in question was last seen piling his gear into a Morris Minor van, never to be seen again. Timbo's case was dismissed because there were no witnesses.

The only good the fracas did for me was that, for weeks after the incident, I was treated with a little more respect. I tried to work out why I had put myself at risk over something that was nothing to do with me. Using brute force was something I thought was tucked away in my dark past, and yet here I was, still capable of behaving in the same old irresponsible manner. Any beak worth his salt would have no second thoughts about putting me out of harm's way for a couple of years at least. I was a sorely troubled man for some weeks after the incident, but the affair died a natural death and I, along with the other lads, consigned it to the history books.

17

Borders and Gun Towers

In early May 1979 I got the news from one of my motorbike chums, a lad called Alex, that the next International Motorcycling Federation rally was to be held in Budapest, during the last week in July. Alex hailed from Ayrshire in Scotland and was one of a group of four of us who had teamed up at the last one in Jönköping.

We made the arrangements: a two-week trek through Germany and Austria, finishing up with a week in Hungary. I agreed to organise the visas at the Hungarian Consulate in Eaton Place in London.

As if on cue, three weeks after my application I got a message on the answer phone: would I ring a number in London and ask for a Mrs Fairbrother and could I do this within the next seven days?

I left it until the last day before I made the call. 'Yes, Mr Gregg, hold on while I put you through to Mr Leftbury.'

As politely as if he were holding an eggshell about to break at any moment, he said, 'Yes, Gregg, we would be obliged if you could suggest a meeting place. We want to send one of our officers down for a chat. We understand that you may be travelling east in the near future. Perhaps we could meet somewhere in Taunton.'

I told him that if they wanted to come down and have a chat there was not much I could do about it, but I put my foot down about meeting in Taunton. 'I don't want to have you or any of your mates like the last pair who turned up at Hinkley Point coming anywhere near my home. If a chat is all you want then I suggest the railway station at Bridgewater would be a much better place.'

It was agreed that the person, whoever he or she might be, was to meet me at Bridgewater. The train pulled into the station almost dead on time, 12.25 p.m. I had taken up position half an hour earlier, sitting in the waiting room, with a clear view of the platform. There he was, obviously not sure of himself, standing on his lonesome.

I slipped out of the back door of the room and sat in the van waiting for him to appear. When he finally came into view I flashed the lights. I could almost feel the relief that swept over the man.

'Thought for a time I was on a wasted journey.'

'Not so far,' I replied. 'I've had you in sights for the last twenty minutes.'

'That follows,' says the man. 'I've read your dossier, including the stuff omitted from your army release documents.'

'Are you referring to my short service with Major Peniakoff? And my work with 14 Military Mission?'

'Yes, Mr Gregg, I am. You are the only one from that group still alive. Perhaps you weren't aware of that.'

'No, it's news to me. When the unit was disbanded we all went our different ways.'

'We understand you are very good at working on your own. It's all there in black and white in the reports.'

'The word "we" suggests to me that there's a gang of you discussing my future.'

He continued. 'To tell you the truth, Mr Gregg, what we don't understand is how a man with your war record and the units you served ended up working with a bunch of Commies. How on earth did that happen?'

I replied that he should never judge people until he was aware of all the facts. I wasn't at all impressed by his starched collar and pinstripe suit; in fact to me he represented the side of authority that was the cause of all my grief. I allowed him to carry on. To give the man his due he did apologise for saying what he did. 'I certainly got off on the wrong foot with that remark.' I gave him a friendly grin and suggested we find a more informal place to continue the discussion. There we were, sitting at a table by the window of an out-of-the way pub on the outskirts of Bridgewater. The man pulled out his wallet and showed me his credentials; they were just the same as those of the couple of goons who had waylaid me up at the Point.

Then I said, 'Now, what about letting me into the secret, from beginning to end! Up till now I'm of the opinion that this is a dress rehearsal for a new production of a Gilbert and Sullivan comic opera.'

'We want you to go back into East Germany, pick up some papers and deliver them to a source in West Germany, that's the beginning and end of it.' This brought my mental faculties to a dead stop.

I got a grip of myself and replied, 'Do you people realise that I'm just a whisker away from my sixtieth birthday? Surely you must have your own specialists for these little junkets.'

'Never mind that. Could you do it?' he persisted.

'Easy enough, but on my own terms, and what's in it for me?'

'Nothing except your expenses, and, by the way, my name is Peter Jones.'

I allowed a glimmer of a smile. 'I'm willing to believe the expenses part but let's drop the Peter Jones rubbish.'

The man grinned and said, 'I think we could consider a figure of five hundred.' I didn't need a calculator to work out that this amount would pay for the whole of the three weeks' holiday.

'Make it six hundred and we might be able to have a discussion. Three hundred before I leave, the rest on delivery.'

I suggested he tell his superiors that the pickup could be in Dresden, Leipzig or Karl-Marx-Stadt in Chemnitz, near where I had been a prisoner of war. 'I exit through the checkpoint at Hof, with a maximum of four days from pickup to delivery, and out of my three suggested points I prefer Dresden as I have a good reason to be in the city.'

The man told me that it was because of my interest in Dresden that British Intelligence had contacted me in the first place. 'Isn't there any place a man can hide?' I asked. Jones just grinned. I named the restaurant at the main crossroad in the centre of Dresden as the pickup point and anywhere between Hof and Nuremberg for the drop. The truth was that I knew these places and felt safer in an area that I was familiar with. I told him that I wanted to do the job in broad daylight. Sometime around midday would suit me well. Jones did not query my stipulation about the rendezvous time but did say that as far as their office was concerned the situation within the DDR was getting a bit precarious and he wondered why I was so certain I could pull it off. I told him I had no intention of putting myself at risk.

'I won't make any move until I am satisfied that the location is clean. If I have suspicions to the contrary then I will just move on, operation over, nothing gained, nothing lost, except, that is, your first three hundred.'

By now me and this lad were on first-name terms. 'The details will be sent in the next few days, Victor.' At first I thought he was a bit immature but then I got to thinking that perhaps this was the way they worked, all palsy-walsy. We parted company like a couple of old friends. Three weeks later a message came through: Peter Jones would be at Bridgewater on the following Tuesday, same place, same time. If I didn't answer, the meet would be taken as confirmed.

By now the doubts that had bothered me during my time at the bank were resurfacing, and I hadn't even done anything except have a meeting. I said nothing to Bett about what had happened. Common sense told me to tell them to stuff it, to find another stooge. I was putting at risk everything that Bett and I had built up together. I decided that I would contact them in the morning and call the whole thing off. After all, what could they do? So, I had wasted the time of a couple of their messenger boys, hadn't fallen in with their line of thinking. I had never been on their staff, my time at the bank had served them well. I had been a useful bagman and information collector, which in fact was the role they were intending me for now, only this time around there was undoubtedly more risk attached, like getting locked up in some manky East German prison.

The next morning and I was still in the business of 'considering'. The thought of the easy six hundred and the old feelings of anticipation made my mind up for me. I swept any doubts aside, knowing that if anything went wrong I would be left to my own devices and have to get myself out of the shit. As always, confidence in my own abilities pushed out any thoughts of failure.

Peter Jones turned up as arranged, the only difference being that this time, feeling like a Boy Scout doing his good deed, I met him as he stepped off the train. Off we went for a drink and something to eat.

The six hundred had been authorised, Dresden had been accepted, the delivery would be at Nuremberg.

'I still cannot for the life of me understand how you people picked an old man like me to do a simple job like this. Surely the government has enough agents on their pay roll without chancing their arm on unknown factors?'

'Rule number one, Victor.' I sense some form of lecture coming and I'm right. 'Never mention the government. Rule number two, there are never enough people to satisfy our needs. Rule number three, feel honoured . . .'

I continued this dialogue. '. . . rule number four, if I'm caught I'm in deep shit.'

Peter gave one of his grins. 'Rule number five, you're dead right.'

He then became serious for a moment. 'You can still refuse, Victor. I can promise you that you will not get any more approaches from the department, but you must tell me now.'

My answer was short and to the point. I was in. Then I said, 'You people know my visa dates – the pickup will have to be a week before I enter Hungary. This will give me time to do the job and then meet up with the rest of my party.'

Peter nodded. 'We'll arrange it.' Then I gave him a lift back to the railway station and that's all there was to it.

The details were finalised after yet another get-together in Bristol, where I was doing some work on the Berkeley nuclear plant. The three hundred was handed over. I didn't even have to sign for it, probably, as I reasoned later, no connection, no responsibility. All I had to do now was to take a trip to London to Berolina Travel to arrange the visa for the DDR.

By Monday of the last week in July, the bike was loaded up with all the paraphernalia that was needed for a two-week camping holiday. Bett waved me off from the front door and in no time I was enjoying the steady reliable throb of an 800cc horizontal twin BMW en route for Dresden and whatever else lay in store for me. I spent the next day in Würzburg and by Wednesday I was setting up camp in a tourist site on the outskirts Dresden which, even more than thirty years after the raid, was still a burnt-out and shattered city. The meeting was set for sometime after three the following afternoon at the restaurant that I had chosen. I set off at about ten the next morning, after a nice shower in the camp washrooms and a change of clothes.

My nerves were tingling, I had an itch in my spine but on the whole I was not unduly worried. Any sign that anything was amiss and I would be on my way, you could say 'hotfooting it for freedom'. Keep your eyes skinned, Vic, I thought to myself, this is not a job for amateurs. The Stasi played for real, or so I had been informed by my friends from the campsite the previous year. I thought back to the days when I had been under Popski's command: 'Always keep a three hundred and sixty-degree surveillance, Gregg. If you ever have to look for a bolthole it will be too late.'

I parked the bike in a special tourist car park and soon I was surrounded by the usual assortment of East Germans, hungry for a look at the latest two-wheeled offering from their counterparts in the west. I pressed a couple of highly illegal western Deutschmarks into the hand of the attendant, with the promise of more to come, and ensured that the bike would be well looked after. Then I made my way to the restaurant which was by the main crossroads in the centre of the city.

The restaurant had two floors, a downstairs bar and coffee counter, and a first floor with seats on an outside balcony from which I could sit at a table and observe the world and its troubles on the pavements below. I took a table, and sat wolfing down a huge cheese roll and supping a beer, preparing for whatever was about to happen.

I had not been supplied with a description of the person I was about to meet. 'Just sit and wait, he will contact you.'

I waited twenty minutes. I had another beer, so far untouched, on the table in front of me. The restaurant was still only about half full, plenty of empty tables. Not surprisingly, I got the odd stare. I stood out like a beacon in my leather jacket, with its Union Jack sewn on the chest and a full complement of badges from all the places I had visited. I must have looked like a Millwall fan in full battle gear, definitely an *Engländer*. I don't think Peniakoff would have approved: he always told me not to draw attention to myself. In trooped a party of young students, kitted out in walking gear. They commandeered a corner of the floor, and like students all over the world they dumped their gear without a thought for the other customers. Soon they were knocking back quart-size glasses of soft drinks and glancing towards me, the stranger in the camp. I heard the usual mutterings of '*Engländer, Engländer*', always in hushed tones as if I was an alien from outer space.

Encouraged by the leader of the group one of the girls came over.

'*Entschuldigen Sie bitte. Sind Sie Engländer?*'

'*Ja, ich bin Engländer,*' I replied.

I was invited to come and join them, whereupon they all started to practise their English. Then the leader explained that he was the English teacher at the local high school where he also taught French and the minor classics (whatever they were!).

'Everyone calls me Bob, otherwise its Robert Halsey, and what do we call you?'

'Victor will do. I'm really waiting for a friend to turn up, but there appears to have been some misunderstanding on his part so I should be on my way.' I thought I should get away from the incessant chattering of these happy-go-lucky young people who were attracting too much attention for my liking.

By this time another beer had been shoved under my nose. The teacher asked me whether I knew the area which he spoke about in the most glowing terms. I said no, I didn't. I was now fully on my guard; the too familiar approach was not natural between strangers, especially in closed societies like the DDR. If this was the contact he was sailing too close to the wind.

Robert asked one of the girls to get a map from his rucksack and then spread it out on the table, and, with the help of much chattering from his pupils, started to describe various beauty spots I might want to visit. By now the whole of the restaurant, including some of the waiters, was extolling the merits of their own particular favourite piece of Saxony acreage to the motorcyclist from England.

'You can keep the map, Victor, I've also put a few notes in an envelope for you. Keep them safe. I'm certain you will find them useful. '*Gehen Sie*, Victor, and good luck. Perhaps we will meet again.' I immediately understood that I was being very discreetly told to get on my way. With handshakes all around I said my goodbyes and left this oasis of goodwill. The envelope I wedged inside my helmet, the map

I left sticking out of my jacket pocket in full view of all and sundry.

I made my way back to the car park, thanked the attendant and, slipping him another couple of illegal western Deutschmarks, made my way back to the campsite. I was sorely tempted to up sticks and away, but sticking to the original plan I sat down in the tent and opened up the map. Out fell a slip of notepaper. There was a message on it saying it was not necessary to go to Nuremberg, but that I could follow the route marked on the map from Hof to Münchberg. The note added that the Gasthof Reitsch did a good lunch, but not before midday. As much as I studied the map I couldn't for the life of me see anything but an ordinary well-used, large-scale map, the type used by walkers the world over. I had never heard of microdots or perhaps there were other ways of concealing information. I studied the map for at least an hour and could not find anything out of the ordinary. As for the envelope, it seemed to be too thin. Whatever it contained must have been very concise and to the point. I didn't open it, just took it out of my helmet and stuck it in the lining of one of my riding boots.

18

The Handover

The following morning saw me on my way to the crossing at Hof. This was not a well-used route into and out of the DDR, but even so it was imposing, even frightening, guarded by watchtowers and machine-gun posts. It gave off an air of dark menace, intimidating to all who had to pass by it. As soon as I left the campsite my instincts told me to dump the map, the note and the envelope. But a sense of curiosity about the unknown grew with every mile I travelled. I slowed and stopped at the barrier wondering whether I would spend the next night in a cell and the rest of my life in Siberia. As it turned out, everything went smoothly, I was waved across the border with only a cursory glance at my passport and in no time I was biking through West Germany, making steady headway towards the small town of Münchberg, which I reached soon after eleven thirty.

The Gasthof Reitsch stood about a hundred yards off the road and having parked the bike and taken off my leathers I made my way into the lounge. Within minutes I was supping what goes for beer in the Fatherland. They call it lager, but to a good Englishman it's polluted tap water. Perhaps that's the reason they have to disguise the taste with lime juice and the like.

'*Engländer?*' said mine host.

'*Ja, ich bin Engländer,*' I reply.

Then, to my astonishment, this worthy says, 'Victor?'

'*Ja, ich heisse Victor,*' I replied, giving the Kraut the benefit of my lowly knowledge of the lingo. He pointed to a table by the window.

'Let's sit down together, Victor, lunch is ordered. I dare say you could do with a bite of decent food.' I rolled myself a cigarette, and for the first time in the last thirty-odd hours I felt at ease. Gone was the tightness of the mind and the necessity of keeping constantly alert. Here in this German wayside hostelry I felt safe, and the comfort of this experience swept through my whole being.

'Now, Victor, while we're waiting for lunch let's see what you've got for me, and, by the way, you can call me Charles.'

I handed over the map, took off my boot and handed over the envelope and the few odd pieces of notepaper. 'That's all I've got.'

'Ah, he's a good man, our Duggie.'

'Duggie?' I said. 'He told me his name was Robert Halsey.'

'You hear a thousand names in this business,' he replied. 'Best thing is to believe all of them or none of them. You take your choice. So you're the new courier then?'

'You're joking,' I replied. 'This is strictly a one-off job, never to be repeated.'

'Time will tell,' he answered and with the business over we both got stuck into the food which had been loaded on to the table. By now I was feeling quite comfortable and once again quite sure of myself. I judged it was time to broach the small matter of payment; after all I had been promised a further three hundred on delivery. I explained this to my new acquaintance who said, 'I've never had to pass over money before. This is news to me.' I must admit that I could see his point, and to be fair I had suspected as much when this method of payment was so readily agreed upon back home. So I said to him, 'I want you to get on to them in London, ask them to get in touch with me in a month's time, after I've got home. But all I want to do now is to get on to Budapest.'

'Not more skulduggery?' said Charles. 'You certainly get around for your age. Don't worry about the cash, I'll get on to London and explain matters.'

With all pleasantries completed, off I went, heading south to my rendezvous with friends I knew I could trust.

That night in a campsite in Austria I had time to contemplate the hare-brained escapade I had involved myself in. It could so easily have gone wrong, and I had no experience of how to get myself out of trouble had something gone wrong.

I knew something about the methods used to get information out of captured agents, and they were pretty gruesome. Years back in 1944, when I was in a prisoner-of-war camp, I struck up a friendship with a lad named Alan who had been captured in North Africa. He told me how, with another prisoner, he had made an attempt to escape. His friend got away but when Alan was recaptured the Germans chained him to a wall in a cellar. The floor of the cellar was under a foot of water. The Germans were convinced that this lad knew where his mate was heading for. There was nothing he could tell them because there had been no plan; he didn't know anything. He was kept in that cellar for four days. The Germans were finally convinced that he knew nothing and returned him to the POW camp. His feet never recovered.

He was still suffering when I was transferred to Dresden. I had no reason to believe that the Stasi prisons would be any more pleasant than the one that Alan had suffered in. I can't really describe my sense of relief that it was all over. Let's just say it felt mighty good.

I had done the job and thought that my relationship with British Intelligence was over. I fell into a deep sleep. All the troubles I had felt hanging over me had gone, cleared as quickly as the morning mist on the distant mountains. All was right with the world. I packed the gear on the bike and headed for Würzburg where I was to meet up with the other lads. They had motored down from Calais, doing the trip in one flying dash. The next morning we would be on the way to Budapest.

That first trip to Hungary was a great success. The rally we were there to enjoy was a huge affair organised by the National Motorcycle Federation of Hungary and was held inside the giant Budapest National Stadium with nearly five thousand enthusiasts from all corners of Europe in attendance. The city council gave out free passes for the public transport system and the citizens of Budapest took us to their hearts. As a bonus there was a huge concert in the stadium featuring the British pop group Queen. They turned up with all the necessary marquees, a couple of dozen huge speakers and an amplifying system that guaranteed that this western rock music would shatter the window panes over half the continent. Everyone agreed that this rally was the best yet.

The holiday over, it was back to the land of Hope and Glory. I was a wee bit subdued for the next few weeks, but my mood soon passed after what I thought was to be the final visit by the men from Whitehall.

Two of them came down to the Point. They wanted to know about all the problems I had encountered and they wrote down my answers. They wanted to get my overall impressions and I told them that I wasn't impressed by the way in which the young students had been used and, while the exercise had gone quite smoothly, I thought they had relied too much on luck. I asked them what they would have done if one member of the system had been compromised or even arrested. How would they have warned me? All the two spooks could do was try and reassure me that 'they' had it all under control. I was not impressed one little bit. Even so my three hundred was handed over, with no signature required. After that I heard no more, the telephone stopped ringing and my spirits returned to normal.

Early the following year I had a call from Alex, one of the three lads who had been with me in Budapest. He wanted the four of us to meet to talk about a return to Hungary. Alex had heard news about the Pannonia International Motorcycle Rally which was one of those rare events where east and west could meet on equal terms. It was sponsored by the National Motorcycling Federation of Hungary and therefore under the control of the authorities. If we could organise the visas all we had to do was make our way to the venue, pay the entrance fee and that would be it. Motorcyclists from all over Europe and Scandinavia were going to be there for the huge five-day event.

What was a fact, though, was that while we in the west could, if we took the trouble, visit any of these gatherings inside the Soviet-controlled areas of Europe, the reverse was true for our friends in the east who were cooped up behind the wire that divided us. Everyone yearned for the day when freedom would once more prevail. When it came to saying goodbye to our friends in the east it was always with a tinge of sadness. One of the lads once said that it was as if we were leaving them trapped in a cage – and he was right.

Alex had all the forms from Hungary sent to his home in Largs. Meanwhile, I went up to Eaton Place to sort out the visas. By the end of May everything was arranged and we were set to leave at the end of June. When I got back, Bett and I decided to go to Spain for three weeks, so everything in the household was on an even keel.

Then I got a message on the answer phone which was terse and to the point – 'they' wanted to meet me, usual place, date and time to be confirmed. 'It would be appreciated.' I was a bit bemused but said I would be there.

Three of them turned up and we met at the pub where we had first encountered each other. To begin with they asked the same questions as the year before and then suddenly one of them said: 'You've applied for another visa for Hungary.' After a pause the leader of the three said, 'No need to look surprised, we get to know these things, and of course taking a trip to the east isn't a crime. We want you to do another trip to the DDR, to Leipzig this time. You've just about time to get down to Berolina and arrange another visa. What about it?'

Well, I thought, talk about getting to the point.

By this time the third man, who was new to me, was showing signs of wear and tear. It was now almost one thirty, nearly two hours into the interview, and this lad had been drinking the local cider while his mates had stuck to the normal insipid lager. Without warning he blurted out, 'I can't see what you're worried about. You must be better than the last man. He managed to get himself picked up.' The other two looked as though they could have shot him on the spot.

'How exactly did the man get picked up? Did he make a mistake? Was he a regular?' It turned out that the idiot had attempted to carry a handgun through the metal detectors at the border crossing. They wouldn't tell me about his length of service except to say that he should have known better. Carrying any form of offensive weapon was a big mistake. My experience had taught me that a bit of blarney can, with luck, get you out of a tight corner. Carrying a gun will more than likely end in disaster.

Looking across the table at these men, I thought that surely writers like John le Carré and company, people who earned their living by spinning tales of deception, of subterfuges carried out in the dark corners of Europe, had never come across the likes of these three. It all seemed totally unbelievable. It did occur to me that possibly they had lost more than one poor sod and were now scraping the barrel to see who else they could find. Raking around their dusty files, some bright spark had discovered me and my evil past. In the end I did the stupid thing and agreed to another run. I still had no idea who I was working for. All they would say was, 'Later, Victor, all in good time.'

I was given an envelope with the instructions and, more pleasing, a bulging envelope containing £300 in cash, with the promise of the same again when I got back. It seemed that £600 was the going rate for this sort of work. I could live with that.

I left on 21 June. I remember the exact date because it was my mum's birthday. I entered East Germany at Hof where, after a cursory glance at my passport and visas, I was waved through. That evening I was ensconced in the tourist *Campingplatz* at Leipzig Nord. The pickup was to take place in a music shop situated on the main *Bahnhofstrasse*. I was to contact a man called Thomas Axster. All I knew about Axster was that he owned a small music shop.

I spent the evening in the campsite swotting up my pigeon Deutsch, *'Ich bin Victor'* and the like, simple phrases that I could use if things went wrong. Never far from the back of my mind was the niggling worry that this time it could all be a disaster. I was travelling in the dark with no idea whether anyone had been compromised. I could have been set up and be walking into a trap. Nevertheless, the old adrenalin was pumping. I found myself gazing into the dusty front window of Musick Axster, in which a couple of cheap looking violins competed with a baby grand piano complete with peeling veneer. I took the bull by the horns and entered this sad looking establishment.

I pushed the door open and a huge brass bell rang somewhere in the depths of the gloom. A pair of velvet curtains at the back of the shop parted and out came an old crone who looked about ninety.

I could not understand a word she said or even follow the rapid German that she came out with. *'Madame, ich bin Engländer. Ich nicht verstehen Deutsch.'* Just as I was beginning to despair she said, 'Ah, you are English' in the type of cultured English that I associated with the nobs back home.

'And what brings you here?'

'I am Victor and I would like to meet with Thomas if he is here?'

Just then the curtains parted again to reveal the said Thomas.

I was invited into a room that reeked of an age long gone. The mantelpiece was covered with a velvet drape in the centre of which was this ancient clock, complete with fancy little turrets. The four corners were fashioned into fluted pillars inlaid with gold leaf. On either side of the clock were family photographs, in heavy old-fashioned frames. It was like being in some ancient palace and, to cap it all, Thomas wore a velvet bell-shaped hat complete with tassel. Time passed and the lady of the house reappeared with a tray of dainty china cups and some English McVitie's biscuits on a plate. They wanted to know why I was going to Hungary, and could I really travel all over the DDR, Poland and all the other countries on their side of the wire? I told them that so long as I obeyed the rules I was allowed to travel anywhere.

I began to think that this elderly English couple (well, at least in my judgement the old lady was English, not so certain about Thomas, definitely of Jewish extraction. But, if so, how had he survived?) were trapped on the wrong side of the Iron Curtain and being used by people who had little regard for their wellbeing. Thomas handed me some sheets of music and a Hohner harmonica, along with a bill of sale for the instrument.

'There you are, Victor, I happen to know that these are not easily obtainable in England today.' He was talking about the Hohner. I knew that these instruments were like gold dust to musicians in the west.

The upshot was that I left the shop with a small bundle of literature, music sheets and a second-hand harmonica. 'The harmonica is yours, Victor, now let me have your camera.' I had a 35mm Nikon which I handed over to him. He wound up the film inside and took the cassette out, replacing it with another cassette which he didn't load.

'There you are, Victor, all safe and sound. You can take the film out as soon as you're free and inside the west. Just act like a tourist and you will be perfectly safe.' And with those parting words of advice I left.

I wanted to get as much distance in the shortest possible time between myself and whatever hanky-panky was going on in the music shop in the *Bahnhofstrasse*. I had to get across the border as quickly as possible.

Back at the tourist *Campingplatz* I had a reasonable evening meal and fell into an uneasy sleep. I worried that if I had travelled straight to the border at Hof I would be safe by now, then I thought, no, if I was in any danger I would have been nabbed as soon as I left the shop. It dawned on me that I was carrying incriminating evidence that could put me away for a very long time. I was suddenly adrift on a sea of self-doubt, something that had not happened to me before. I approached the check point with my heart beating like a jack hammer and my palms sweating. I needn't have worried – I was waved through with hardly a glance and all was right with the world.

The next morning I was back at the Gastof Reitsch. There I found a note from the gentleman who had told me to call him Charles saying he was sorry for the delay but would be at the Gastof early next morning. There was nothing for it but to order a hearty meal and get tucked up with a book. In all of my travels I have never failed to have a book handy for situations like this. The chap who ran the place said that he would put the bike in his garage. He showed me to my room and in the blink of an eye I was in the land of nod. Charles turned up the next morning while I was wolfing down a huge German breakfast.

'Thought you weren't going to do any more.'

The same grin. He settled the bill and we got on with the business in hand while supping some of the local brew. I put the stuff the old man had handed me on the table.

'That's just what we need,' said Charles as he pocketed the small can of 35mm film. 'Have another beer, Victor, you've done a good job.' Then he said, 'Surely you didn't do the pickup dressed up like you are now?' He meant my colourful leathers.

'Who's going to suspect me of doing anything underhand dressed up like a lighthouse?'

'Better you than me,' he answered. I changed the subject, trying to find out more about what was going on.

'Just how extensive is this Saxony cell?'

'I can't talk to you about that sort of thing, Victor, I've only been here for a year and a half but there's been no trouble as yet.'

'You surprise me,' I answered, thinking about the amateurish way it appeared to be organised, at least in my experience. And that was about it. I was getting nowhere so I said my goodbyes and pointed the bike in the direction of Budapest and set off to join my mates at the rally.

It must have been late in November that I received a letter with the logo of the Ministry of Information on the envelope. They wanted me to come to London. The address was a room in the big office block in Hart Street, opposite Bloomsbury Square. I knew this building from the past. I had worked on it when it was being built in the 1960s and it was now 1983 and I had just celebrated my sixty-fifth birthday. Anyhow, always ready for a laugh and an excuse to have a day in the Smoke, I phoned through my agreement.

I presented myself the following week and was directed by a uniformed guardian up to the fourth floor where I found that, once out of the lift, there was only one door. While I wondered what to do next the door opened, I was ushered in and invited to 'take a pew'. The room had the appearance of a hospital surgery: a couple of standard-issue metal filing cupboards, a six-foot wooden table, a few chairs and not even a telephone. The woman who had opened the door looked down at the notes on her desk and then said: 'You are Mr Victor Gregg? Major Gardiner will be in directly. Would you like a coffee?' I accepted this offer with as much good grace as I could muster. Just as well, as the 'directly' turned out to be about half an hour.

The so-called 'Major' Gardiner came in and apologised for keeping me waiting. I kept a straight face. He was completely different from the lightweights I had been dealing with so far. He had the air of a senior army officer and the accent to go with it and, naturally, he was polite in the extreme. At last I had come face to face with someone in authority.

I asked him whether he was surprised that his men had chosen such an elderly and unknown person for such tricky work.

'Not in your case, Mr Gregg. I've been through your files, I've read everything from the day you signed on all those years ago. You have more than justified our decision to use you. You haven't put a foot wrong.' He handed me a piece of notepaper with an address printed on it. 'If you ever need to get in touch with me you can do so by writing to this address or, in an extreme emergency, by using the telephone number.' Long experience warned me that I was getting the full treatment, the blarney was hitting from all angles. Watch it, Vic, the hammer blow is about to be launched at any moment.

I was never more wrong in my life. He asked me about the various campaigns I had been involved with, what made me move to the Para Regiment, and what did I consider to be the hardest of the battles, all the usual stuff.

The interview ended on good terms. It seemed to me that the major just wanted to see at first-hand what sort of an idiot I was. I hope he satisfied himself. For my part I had already decided that all the bullshit in the world would not persuade me to carry on these expeditions. I could almost smell the dangers and risks involved. On the way out I was handed an envelope by the secretary. It contained £300 and a letter of thanks from Gardiner. This time I had to sign for it. That was the only time I actually met any person of authority in the Ministry. The address the major had given me was in some department of the Foreign Office, exactly which one I never found out. Anyway, at last it was all done with. I was free.

And so back to Taunton and the everyday slog of earning a living. How I hated the mind-numbing dreariness of the daily grind.

The following May, Bett and I had three glorious weeks in France. There were none of the petty restrictions I'd come across in Britain. Find a nice river, set up the tent, get the fishing tackle out and no bailiffs threatening to confiscate your tackle. I love the easy-going manner with which the French people go about their lives. Just keep clear of breaking the speed limit, try to obey the local bye-laws and be as free as a bird. If only I could speak the lingo; it's not that I haven't tried, I've bought correspondence courses, even gone into Smith's and come away with *Simple French in a Week*. I've tried the lot, but to no avail.

We got back home to find the usual pile of letters stacked up behind the front door. Among all the bills and final demands was a brown envelope stating quite clearly that it was from the Ministry of Information.

'What do they want with you, Vic?'

'Oh, it's not important, love, it's probably something about that job at the Point.'

I was really annoyed at them for contacting me at home. So far I had kept everything secret from Bett. All she knew was that I had been away with my friends, something which she encouraged. And it's true that I always appreciated my home much more after I had been away, especially as the four of us really roughed it on our trips. More often than not the night's bed-down would be under a hedge on some lonely lane away from habitation. The way we went about our holidays certainly wasn't everyone's cup of tea.

I opened the letter to find they wanted me to phone this number within the next couple of days, and they gave a name for reference – so much for my new freedom. Very reluctantly I rang and arranged a meeting. I was on the hook, my adrenalin boiling. It turned out they wanted me to contact a person in Magdeburg. They even had a date.

This was an area of the DDR about which I knew nothing. I jibbed, but yet again failed to stand my ground. The big obstacle this time would be explaining to Bett why I wanted to go to East Germany so early in the year. There was no way I could let on about the true nature of the trip; she would have put her foot down with the same firmness as her ancestors at Bannockburn. For the first time I would have to lie to her and this caused me pain, but lie I did. My explanation to Bett was that Henry, the fourth member of our squad, was returning from Poland and I used this as an excuse to meet him on the border near Dresden. The truth was that Henry was already back in dear old Blighty.

Once more I thought about my life. I had now reached the ripe age of sixty-five and in the course of a working week I was clambering up two hundred-foot-high electricity pylons, keeping an eye on the lads I was employing and always with their safety in mind. I made it a point never to ask any man to get into a situation that I had not previously tried out myself. What we did was paint the pylons, which was like painting the Forth Bridge only not so easy. We climbed up, tied a rope and pulley to whatever bit of the gantry we were on and let it down to a lad on the ground who would send up tins of priming paint.

We worked in teams of six and each man had to tie a gallon tin of this heavy paint to his thigh and then, hand over hand, work himself to the far edge of the structure where he could start laying on the paint, thick and heavy, always working his way back to the centre. The Electricity Generating Board used to cut the power from the half that we would be working on and at the slightest hint of moisture in the air we would be grounded. In damp weather you could see and hear the electric flashes as the power jumped from the live lines to the dormant half of the pylon. The safety harness was a rope tied around the waist tied to a sliding noose attached to the steelwork, the trouble being that it was too easy to get yourself tangled up. This meant that most of the lads, myself included, used to dispense with the safety option and just rely on keeping a firm grip on the steelwork. We all knew the dangers, but the money was out of this world. In the five or so years that I was engaged I never heard of a fatality in any of the half-dozen teams that worked the South West. I had an ageing Land Rover that I kept at the Point especially for these jobs. I knew that in the South West there were no more than forty-odd men capable of doing this sort of work.

Now there was this letter from the ministry. It suggested that the meeting be held at what I now thought of as our office – the pub called the Cottage. When we met I opened proceedings by venting my wrath on the lot of them for sending the letter to my home. They tripped over themselves with their apologies.

'It was a mistake at the office.'

'What office?' As usual they didn't rise to the bait. I was still in the dark as to who these men were working for.

They gave me a map of the city of Magdeburg and said that in due course I would be given the time, date and place of the pickup. They promised that simplicity would be the keyword. We all kept off the local brew, we said our good-byes and I was left to think over what I should do next, if anything.

I arranged to meet with Henry the coming weekend; he knew a thing or two about life behind the Iron Curtain. After the usual chit-chat I asked him if he had ever been through Magdeburg. His response was sharp and to the point.

'Why do you want to go to that hole, Vic? It's the biggest industrial shithouse in the whole of the DDR, and what's more the place is crawling with police and the bastard Stasi. They'll run you in just for blinking at them.' Henry was not a man to mince his words.

'Not me, Henry, it's just that someone was asking about the place, nothing to do with me.'

The next day I was on the phone to the major, who, naturally, was not in the building. I left a message that I was to be contacted within the next twenty-four hours.

Which I was, not by the major, but by some underling who I had never met. I gave him the reference number the major had given me and in no time at all he was tuned in.

'Right then, Mr Gregg, tell me the problem. I'm assuming by your tone that you've got one.' I told him there was no way that I was going to meet anyone in or near Magdeburg. I was willing to do the business at the railway station at

Schönebeck, which was about thirty miles south of Magdeburg, and that was the best I could offer. 'Leave it with me, Mr Gregg. Someone will get back to you.'

The next lot of instructions arrived by letter just over a week before their deadline. I phoned Berolina Travel and managed to get the visa on a hurried trip to London the following day. I said that I was doing research into the Dresden bombing. This went down well with the people at Berolina who knew what had happened there.

The obvious route into East Germany to get to Magdeburg was via the crossing at Helmstadt, following the main E30 Autobahn. The motorway follows the southern route to Berlin especially to accommodate the ancient city of Magdeburg. But that was too obvious for me. Instead I made my way down to Würzburg to the local *Campingplatz* where I was on speaking terms with the old lady who owned the site. I had first met her when I took my younger boy to Yugoslavia all those years ago.

Those visits usually ended with me sitting among the family for the evening meal, any attempt to pay my way ending with a firm refusal. They would not take my money. These were very good people.

From Würzburg I pointed the bike east towards the little township of Meiningen, stopping for the night at a small tourist *Campingplatz* outside Erfurt. It was there that two men in civilian clothing with a policeman in attendance asked me to produce my documents. I wasn't the slightest bit worried, I knew that my documents were in order in every respect.

Next they told me to unload all my gear from the bike. Part of this included two bottles of whisky and two hundred English cigarettes. I laid everything out by the side of the road in a neat and regimental manner. I knew all about kit inspections. This little episode ended up with them opening one of the bottles and making heavy inroads into the fags. In half an hour all four of us were on the best of terms. *Engländers* carrying Scotch whisky and decent coffin nails were the flavour of the day.

They explained that the authorities had been alerted by the unusually large number of visa entries in my passport and that from their angle they wondered why a westerner would want to travel to the east when everyone in the east wanted to travel west. Investigation was called for. I told them about being in Dresden at the time of the terror bombing and how I made a pilgrimage to that city every year. In no time they were saying their piece about how wrong war was and how we should all be friends, forgetting how enthusiastic their fathers had been when Hitler started it all. With much slapping of backs the four of us went our separate ways. I did wonder whether this had been a sort of warning shot across my bows.

The next day, after a somewhat sleepless night in a field off the main drag, I arrived at the rendezvous. I was thirty minutes early. The town was larger than it seemed on the map. Wednesday must have been market day. Outside the station yard stalls were laid out with farm produce, people aimlessly milling around, just like market places anywhere. Except there was none of the hustle and bustle you normally find at these events – no stallholders shouting their wares, none of those gaudy bundles of balloons tethered to long pieces of string. Everything on offer except the fruit and veg seemed to have been handed down and reused, passing from one owner to the next. An old woman near me had a blanket laid out on the ground covered with bundles of rusty nails, obviously straightened after much use. It was all like that but it didn't matter. I had other things on my mind.

Here I was dressed up to the nines in my expensive leathers, with the latest bike from the BMW factory in the west and I stood out like a lighthouse, a blaze of colour and a reminder of what these people were missing. The bike and I soon became the centre of attraction, which was no good at all.

At the entrance to the station was a small police kiosk, with three lads on duty. I wheeled the bike over and with the usual combination of my limited lingo and a lot of arm waving I persuaded them to keep an eye on it while I went walkabout, handing them as a reward the now half-empty bottle of Scotch. These uniformed lads were not like the police in Britain. They didn't appear to have the same authority. It occurred to me that being a policeman to them was just a job; they left all the nasty work to the hated Stasi.

It was now well past the time for the rendezvous. I imagined that whoever was going to make contact was lurking somewhere, watching me; either that, or something had gone wrong. I bought a couple of what looked like the remains of last year's apple crop and sat down on a bench to have a munch, a quiet smoke and to await developments. I waited an hour in that market. If those clowns in London thought I was going to put myself at risk, hanging about for some Kraut to appear, then they had another thing coming. They had paid me and hard luck for them if they had wasted their money.

Enough was enough. I went over to the lads who were looking after the bike, one of whom was sitting astride the machine living in some Walter Mitty land of dreams. I thanked them profusely, indicating that they could keep the rest of the bottle and handing over a few more of the fags.

Then with a wave to the admiring throng, I gave the township the benefit of seeing my rear wheel disappearing in the distance as I headed for Dresden.

A couple of weeks after I got back two gents came down to Bridgewater and agreed that I had done the right thing. Whoever it was they were dealing with had lost contact, possibly because it had become too difficult to operate, or, worse, because they had been rounded up. I was never contacted again, and that finally, and at long last, was the end of my involvement with the nation's intelligence officers. I never did find out who they really were.

19

The Awakening

Something had changed in me. I realised this one day sitting down with the lads, enjoying the midday lunch break. It's a moment that I shall never forget. We were working on a cheese factory near Taunton. Bronco had turned up for work on a huge farm horse which he tethered in a field at the back of the factory. Some of the lads, including me, were trying to climb on the beast's back. Bronco was shouting encouragement: 'It's only a bloody horse, mount up and give 'im a kick.' But, one after the other, we slithered to the ground. I suddenly realised that I was free from the anger and torture of the past twenty years or so. I still had my hatred and mistrust of authority but here I was, laughing and joking and really enjoying the company of those around me. Bronco and his unique method of transport will be with me for evermore.

I think that the start of my return to some sort of sanity came when I questioned the brutal part I had played in the business of Timbo and his estranged wife. I knew full well the dangerous nature of the blow that I had landed in that soft part of that lad's cranium right behind his ear, but I had still thrown the punch that could have ended in the chap's death.

The realisation that I had the potential to be a murderer forced me to look at myself more deeply than I had ever done. I had been to the brink and looked into the abyss. At that moment I understood the sort of man I had been and the hurt I had inflicted on those I loved and cherished. After the divorce from Freda I thought I had conquered my deranged mind. The affair at Timbo's house proved me wrong. Freda had once said, 'I can't remember the last time I heard you laugh.' Well, I had been laughing and joking a lot during these last few months. I found myself able to accept things I didn't agree with and make a joke of it. Sometimes I would look at my Bett and feel that I was capable of flying like a bird. For the very first time since my demobilisation I began to view the future in a new light. The luck that had kept me alive during the terrible battles of the war was now with me in my battle with life.

My three motorbike mates and I still went every year to Hungary. The trips had become part of our routine. We had come into contact with a small group who were part of a larger group called the 'Democratic Forum'.

It was on a follow-up trip to visit Marcus at Schneefeld that he arranged for his Uncle Albert to meet me. When we at last came face to face I immediately recognised him: this was old Silverhair, the German officer who had been put in charge of us paratroopers when we were captured after the Battle of Arnhem. It would be hard to forget the sight of that one-armed officer, one leg heavily bandaged, balancing with a stick and acting with absolute authority. 'Some geezer that,' we all agreed. Later he had turned up in charge of our work camp. The amazing thing about him was that he spoke perfect English with a Yorkshire accent. It turned out his mother was from that part of England while his father was from Saxony. I remember him warning us not to make any trouble. 'You red-headed bastards banged me up good and proper so I've been sent to keep you in order and that's what I intend to do.' The red-headed bit was a reference to our red berets and he smiled when he said it. We prisoners realised that he was paying us a compliment, that he admired us, soldier to soldier. The last time I had seen him was on my last day at the work camp, the day before I was arrested and condemned to death for sabotaging the soap factory we were toiling in. This was the same man, Albert Jünger.

Herr Jünger did not recognise me until I reminded him who I was and the circumstances of our last acquaintance. The penny dropped and he said: 'I never expected to see you alive again.'

I told him what had happened at Dresden, how the bombing had destroyed the execution prison I was being held in and how I had stayed in the burning ruins for five days before escaping. He then told me that at the POW camp a report had come in saying that my sentence had been carried out, and that I had been executed by firing squad. It was all a long time ago and meeting this man again was one of the strangest coincidences of my life.

That first evening the three of us, myself, Marcus and Albert, walked to the village where I was introduced to a number of Albert's ex-army comrades. Later, we enjoyed another evening of schnapps and the ubiquitous German pork sausages, finally wending our way home in a comradely drunken stupor. We talked about the political situation in Hungary and I described the growing unrest in Poland, which was news to them. It seemed that trouble was brewing in Eastern Europe.

As we parted company at the end of the evening Albert Jünger said to me: 'Tell your friends in Hungary that never again will the German army (he meant the East German army) support any more adventures like Prague.' He was referring to the way the German soldiers had been used by the Soviets to crush the Czechoslovakian uprising in 1968. He was deadly serious. In Saxony at least the general population had had their fill of the way the baleful influence of the Russians blighted their lives.

The following year, when we went to the Pannonia, I mentioned this conversation to our friends in Hungary. I think this was almost the first time that word had filtered down that the East Germans might be in support of action against the Soviet Union. It was especially important that the information had come from a veteran German officers' group. My friends could hardly contain their excitement.

I was asked if it would be possible for me to arrange a meeting between a small group of the Hungarian Democratic Forum and Albert and his colleagues. They said it would be much appreciated. I pointed out that as Albert was old and not well, and unlikely to be able to travel, they would have to go to him.

'No problem, Victor. You fix up a meeting and we will get there.'

Back in the camp that evening the lads were worried.

'Surely you're not going to get involved with this, Vic. They shoot people over here for messing about with politics.' I didn't tell them what I had been up to since our meeting up at Jönköping in Sweden. If I had I am pretty sure they would have dropped me like a ton of bricks.

So instead of going straight home from the rally I returned to Hof, arranged a transit visa to Dresden, and from there went on to Schneefeld, where I made contact with Albert and he agreed to discuss everything with his old cronies as soon as he could. He said he was going to write and invite me to visit him, but apart from that nothing should be put on paper. We both knew that we were dipping our feet into murky waters. 'I think it better that you should stay clear of Marcus and the family until this is all over,' he said. I agreed. I suggested that I come over the following Easter, but that I would keep him advised by adding a few words on a Christmas card. We had another drinking session that evening and I returned to the safety of British shores. 'Don't expect too much,' was Jünger's parting comment.

All this news I put in a letter to a woman called Marlais, the only person I knew in the Hungarian group who had a reasonable command of English. Scarcely two weeks later she wrote back saying my news had generated some excitement. Could I manage to get to Dresden as early in the New Year as possible? She said it was important that contact was made quickly with my friends in the DDR.

I promised to try to arrange a meeting for the following May. I realised that yet again I was getting up to my old tricks; this time there would be no payment and the consequences of discovery didn't bear thinking about.

While Hungary was by far the most easy-going of the so-called Eastern Democracies, in countries like Czechoslovakia, Bulgaria, and of course the DDR itself things were different. The fear that people in those places were subjected to as they went about their daily routines could be felt in the atmosphere. The unhappiness of the people in the streets said it all. They weren't good places to spend a holiday.

Before every Christmas Bett and I used to go round the winter sales in Taunton buying stuff like clothes, soap and even toilet rolls to send to Marcus, his family and friends. They were short of these things and the parcels were much appreciated. One year we sent his two girls American-style jogging suits which went down especially well. It made us proud to be British when we got their letters of thanks saying how wonderful it must be to live in the United Kingdom.

By now Freda had married a chap who gave her all the encouragement and love that I, to my everlasting shame, had failed to supply. His devotion had enabled her to go through college and she was now well respected in her chosen profession. My son David thought that the parting of the ways had enabled Freda and me to find our true way in life. 'Do you think she could have gone through college if you had still been together?'

He had a point and he meant well, trying to help me forget the past, but it only made me feel worse. Had I really been such a swine? To my way of thinking the answer was yes. Anyway, cutting out all that guilt stuff, the children were now married and supplying me with grandchildren, many times over.

I occasionally suffered the nightmares – people burning in the street, flames reaching down from the heavens like huge claws, women flying in the air, their heads on fire, and worst of all the terrible tunnel from which I could never seem to escape. I have often woken bathed in sweat with the sound of terrible screams ringing in my ears.

Later I got a letter from Marlais asking me to write to Albert. Four of them were proposing to be in Karl-Marx-Stadt, in Chemnitz, the small town near Dresden, on 1 June and could I get things organised? I wasn't too happy about using the postal service. I wondered what would happen to Albert and his friends if any of the letters were intercepted. I decided that once again I would have to act as courier. But how was I going to disguise what I was up to? I had no reason now to travel behind the Iron Curtain. There were no rallies to act as an excuse.

I solved the problem by putting my occupation in my passport as historian. If questioned I could talk about my interest in the history of Dresden. In any case it didn't seem to me that I would be in any danger. I was visiting friends, and I wasn't carrying any incriminating documents because everything was verbal.

There were problems, though. Every visit to the DDR would be stamped in my passport; too many visits and the authorities would be alerted that I was up to something. Then I got another letter from Marlais enclosing another letter in German which she wanted me to hand over to 'my friends', meaning, of course, Albert and his cronies.

The letter had raised the stakes. Carrying it into the DDR turned the adventure into a form of Russian roulette. Supposing there was a police, or, worse, a Stasi, reception committee? These thoughts didn't make for some sound nights' sleep. I knew, too, that Marcus and his wife were getting uneasy about my liaison with Albert. They knew that something was afoot but had no idea what. What I did know was that one false move could place me and possibly Albert and all his companions in extreme danger.

Albert seemed to have no qualms about his own safety, and was much more worried about the possibility of me getting picked up. Once he asked me why I didn't settle down and stop living on the edge. 'You got away with it once, next time you may not be so lucky.' I decided after the first trip on behalf of the Hungarian group that Uncle Albert was right – it was in the best interests of Marcus and his family to cut contact with them completely.

It was clear that Albert and his cronies knew perfectly well that the Hungarians were cooking something up and that whatever it was they could have a lot of influence. I

came to the conclusion that these Wehrmacht veteran officers' groups carried a lot of weight in the army of the DDR,
and loyalty is a big thing with soldiers everywhere.

Just as I had been trained to do I made every move in
broad daylight and in the open. Not for me the skulking in
dark alleyways under a dimly lit lamp. I was there for all to
see, cracking a joke with the police and the Stasi. I think this
helped me survive on more than one occasion.

20

Free at Last

It was now 1988, a year short of my seventieth birthday. Our small group of four motorcyclists: myself, Henry who lived in Dorset, Tom and Alex who lived in Scotland, met at our favourite British campsite at Hayfield in Derbyshire to talk about what we were going to do for the rest of the year. Early in May Henry had returned from another trip to his beloved Poland and reported the growing unrest there. We planned a trip to have a week in the Tatra Mountains, on the borders of Poland and Czechoslovakia, before going on to Hungary for the annual Pannonia Rally. The other three were going to set off in the last week of July. I was to leave a week earlier to join some German friends in Dresden before meeting with Albert. I could now speak fairly good German and had even taken a course at our local college.

When I finally made it to Albert I told him what Henry had said about things in Poland. I got the feeling that they were starved of news and that our friends in Hungary were playing their cards very close to their chests. There didn't seem to be much trust yet. It was then that I suggested that their enslavement to the Soviet Union might not last through the next twelve months.

On this last visit to Dresden I had arranged to meet up with Albert on the Tuesday afternoon in the usual café with the balcony. So there I was, drinking my coffee when, without so much as a by your leave, two smartly dressed individuals plonk themselves down in two of the three vacant chairs. I hoped they wouldn't notice my sweaty brow. They asked me who I was. I told them my name and produced my passport.

'*Ach so, Engländer. Sprechen Sie Deutsch?*'

'No, can't speak a word, mate.'

After a few enquiries about why I was in the DDR and mundane words about the weather they got up and left. Normal breathing was again resumed. This proved to me that things were hotting up. 'Be careful, Vic,' I muttered to myself. On that occasion nothing else happened and I got home safe and sound.

At the end of March I got a letter from Budapest asking if I could set up a meeting in Dresden. I replied saying I did not think this was a good idea and that I would have to think about it. In the end I agreed to visit the city one more time, possibly in June, and that they should let me know what they wanted. Within ten days I had their reply and a bundle of questions, all in German.

Even though I reckon Bett believed that I had a bit on the side in Dresden I managed to get her blessing for the trip. This time I did not contact Albert in advance. I would do that when I got there and when I thought it was safe to do so. When I reached the campsite everything seemed to have calmed down, or maybe it was me who was a bit less tense. I posted off a letter to Albert asking if he could meet me. I had three days of wandering around Dresden before I got a letter from him saying that he would come to the site. He was making it easy for me.

When he arrived he told me that there had been demonstrations in Leipzig and Karl-Marx Stadt and that the security services of these two cities had been reinforced by drafts of the army and police from the quieter areas of Saxony, including Dresden. Albert also told me that for the first time the police used dogs on long leashes instead of the more usual water cannon. Albert didn't believe these demonstrations would amount to much and thought that before anything was achieved blood would have to flow. I asked him if there had been any more meetings with the Hungarians. 'None that I'm aware of,' he answered. 'You can put your head above the parapet, Victor, here we have to be more careful.'

Then I gave Albert the letters and stuff from Budapest. I said that I didn't have a clue what it was all about, that they had wanted to come to Dresden and that I had put them off. I also said that to my mind something was going to happen this year and that it was obvious that they were trying to drum up support from him and his cronies.

'You've got it partly right, Victor, but all they have asked us for is information about troop movements and the state of affairs between the state and the army. You ask my opinion, I think they're going to stage some form of uprising. We naturally encourage that although we don't think they stand a chance. This stuff you've just given me is asking whether the East German army would allow itself to be sent through Czechoslovakia into Hungary to help deal with any trouble. I've answered in two words: not possible.'

With that he handed me back the papers. At that moment we were joined by three men; one I recognised from previous meetings with Albert and his mates, the other two, better dressed, were new to me. I nearly choked into my beer as Albert introduced the stranger as a friend of his and said that he was an officer in the Stasi.

The stranger smiled and offered his hand but gave no indication of his name. 'Victor, listen carefully. You will stay in your *Campingplatz* for this night, tomorrow you will leave the DDR by the border crossing at Hof. You must not go through until after 1.30 p.m. and before 4 p.m.' This was translated by Albert who didn't seem to be worried. As for me, I was shitting bricks. I left for the campsite as per instructions, complete with the incriminating evidence stuffed into my pockets. I prayed that Albert's trust in the Stasi officer was justified.

I sailed through the crossing at Hof without anyone giving a damn who I was and where I was going. A couple of kilometres into the west, I anchored up and sat down on the grass verge and puffed away at three fags on the trot. I was shaking like a leaf.

I posted everything off to Marlais as soon as I got to home ground. With it I put a letter saying that no further attempts should be made to get in touch with any of their contacts in the DDR.

I decided to do one more favour for the British Establishment: I phoned the number that had been given me by the major in Hart Street. I told them that if they sent a man down I would give them a report on matters that might be of interest. Two weeks later I was visited by another unknown and I handed over twelve typewritten pages containing everything I knew except the names of my friends.

'You're a bit of a dark horse,' he said.

'Just doing my little bit to help a few friends,' I answered.

He thanked me and said I was telling them stuff about which they had not been aware. He asked me if I was certain that everything I had written down was true. I told him that all I knew was that something was going to happen soon, most likely before the end of the year. I heard nothing more from them.

At the beginning of July the four of us each received a letter from Marlais pleading with us to make it to the next Pannonia Rally. She said it was important and that we should make a special effort to be there. We all met up in Würzburg a week or so later, prior to the final leg of the journey to Sopron in Hungary where that year's rally was being held. When we arrived on 16 July Marlais and her husband were already there, along with some of our acquaintances from Poland and East Germany, including a strong contingent from Berlin.

The town of Sopron stands on the border with Austria, just south of Vienna. On 18 July we were contacted by our Hungarian friends and told to look out for the notices that were soon going to appear all over the town. Sure enough, before evening began to cast its shadows, small posters went up, stuck on lampposts, mail boxes and the walls of houses. The police took no notice of them, which was surprising, because the posters were advertising a 'Picnik' to be held outside of the town and organised by the Magyar Party for Democracy which became better known as the Pan-European Union and the Hungarian Democratic Forum. During the evening the town continued to fill up with people from all over the east – Poles, Czechoslovakians, Bulgarians and, most obvious of all, the East Germans.

The nineteenth arrived, baking hot, which is what it was normally like at that time of year. Around midday we started to make our way to the site of the Picnik. Everybody in the city seemed to have the same idea. When we arrived we made contact with our friends who had a long table fixed up underneath a huge banner carrying the slogan 'PICNIK SOPRONBAN!' and in smaller letters 'MAGYAR

DEMOCRATIC FORUM', plus more information in Hungarian that we couldn't begin to understand.

In the middle of the field the activity was centred around a huge pot of goulash, simmering over a blazing fire. In charge of this was no less a figure than the Mayor of Sopron himself, a jovial roly-poly man as round as he was tall. There he was stirring at the pot which must have contained about twenty gallons of stew. Soon large helpings were being dished out to the accompaniment of an accordion.

Then we saw that at the edges of the field people were cutting down the barbed wire fence, even though they were overlooked by tall forbidding watchtowers equipped with heavy machine guns, each tower about five hundred metres from the next. What was strange was that the towers were unmanned. I had never seen this before. We were told that this first wire barrier was only the first, minor fence. The main border wire was two kilometres away and was going to be cut at three in the afternoon. They wanted us to get to it as soon as possible. One of our group had a heart problem, another was suffering from a slightly sprained ankle, so it was left to myself and the fourth member of the team, Mark, our other friend from the Isle of Wight, to make the walk to the scene of the action. Up to then we had been with a couple of Germans but they didn't want to join us. There were a couple of news crews filming the scene and our new friends were frightened of possible reprisals if they were caught on camera, which was understandable we thought.

We were told that we were going to be given the privilege of joining the group who were to make the first cut in the main border wire. Why us, I wanted to know? We had no part to play in this historic occasion. I was told in no uncertain terms that without the certainty that the East

German military would not get involved it would have been difficult to get the support from the general public. It was the contact we had made with Albert and his veterans that had helped them decide to go ahead, and they were grateful. I felt very honoured by this. After all, what were we? Just a group of working-class lads who liked motorbikes, and yet they made me feel that in some small way we had helped their cause.

We set off over the fields and along a muddy lane. For the last few hundred metres there were the cars of the East Germans, dumped by the roadside. I noticed two camera crews, one of which I think was French. Mark and I were handed a pair of wire cutters and there and then we added our cut, along with hundreds of others.

On the other side of the wire, standing around trying their best to look official, were the Austrian border guards. A human wave of happy and excited people flung themselves out of the confines of no man's land and into the arms of the west. I heard later that the initial number of two hundred had risen to seven hundred. I have no way of knowing the true figures. Eventually Mark and I trudged back to the main field where we had time to reflect on the enormity of the event we had been privileged to have taken part in.

We stayed for the rest of the week. Tom and Alex were going back via Berlin to keep company with some of the East German contingent. It came through later that the DDR had stopped all further travel of its nationals through Czechoslovakia from the north. This was their swan song as it turned out. As for me, I made it back on my own to Dover.

The four of us made another trip to Budapest the following year. By then everything had altered, seemingly for the worse. The streets were dirtier, and the whole city looked as though it was in chaos and on the edge of anarchy.

When the four of us met up again at our annual meet at the campsite in Derbyshire I asked if they had heard anything from Marlais – nothing. We thought this was strange. I wrote to her, but I never received a reply. I often think about Marlais and her friends who seem to have vanished off the face of the earth. I wonder what happened to these brave individuals.

Some weeks after my return from our last trip to Hungary I was coming home one evening from the Point. It had been an easy day and I was driving the bike at a nice slow pace. Three fire engines and an ambulance passed me heading towards Bridgewater. Then I saw smoke ahead. It was one of these olde English farmhouses. The thatch roof was a mass of flame, with sparks jumping all along its length, and as I slowed up to pass the scene I saw the body of a woman hanging from one of the top windows. She was obviously dead but her hair and clothing were well alight. I passed, without even slowing down. Much later that evening Bett said, 'You're as white as a sheet, Vic, what's the matter?'

'Got a bit of a headache, Bett. I'm off up to bed, early night, like.'

'I'll pop up with a cup of tea in a moment.'

And that was the last I knew for the next four days. When I finally came to I learned that I had spent those four days and three nights swearing and screaming. My temperature had risen to 104. A doctor had visited from the local hospital and two nurses who had taken turns to watch over me had just left.

Two days later the doctor visited me and I told him about the fire I had seen on the way home from work. I also told him the story of Dresden and how it had affected me. For the next month or so I had to endure the well-meaning efforts of various specialists. What none of them knew was that I had been cleansed. The nightmares are a thing of the past, the way I behave to others, the apparent rudeness, the brutality, all gone. I feel free, I can laugh, people can take the mickey out of me and I can join in the joke, whatever it's about. I think what finally did it was the sight of that poor woman, hanging lifeless out of that top window, her clothes and hair alight.

My future trips out of Britain were confined to camping trips to France and the occasional hated package trip, to Spain, Corfu, Cyprus and the like. Bett loves those trips. Get in a taxi, an hour to the airport, two or three hours in the plane and there you are, no hassle, just the job she says, so I give in gracefully and make sure she enjoys herself. My business failed on my sixty-sixth birthday due to the fact that a main contractor for whom I was doing work went bankrupt and left me owing many thousands of pounds.

After my bankruptcy I suggested to Bett that it might be a good thing to move up to Scotland where she would be near her sisters and her mum. We finished up in a small town near Morpeth in Northumberland but it turned out to be too cold for Bett so off we went again, ending up in South Wales on a mobile home site. We were completely at peace with the world in this tiny Welsh-speaking village and we stayed for almost ten years before our final move to Winchester.

Ever since Bett and I moved out of the London area I had made a point of keeping in touch with Freda and the children. At least once every three or four months I would aim the bike towards Farnborough where Freda and Joe, her husband, now lived. I was always made welcome and Freda and I would exchange an embarrassed kiss and a hug. I am certain that Joe, along with Bett, understood that there would always be a link between Freda and myself that time would never destroy.

Joe was the first to go. Bett and I went to his funeral. We paid our respects but we didn't stay for the reception and made our way back to South Wales in silence.

Months later my daughter Judith told me that Freda had cancer but said that it was all in hand and that there was nothing to worry about. But that wasn't true. Freda passed away in January 1999 and it left me grief-stricken. I was with her on her last evening. She was upstairs in her bedroom. We could hear the family below nattering away. I laid down beside her and held her hand while she lay there, drifting in and out of consciousness. I know that both of us were going back through the past, Freda suffering the agony that was taking her life away and myself full of guilt. It was as if we both knew that we had thrown something very precious away. I was clinging to her hand, and she said to me, 'Where did it all go wrong, Vic?' I had no answer, only a deep feeling of shame.

Then Freda saved me from having to answer by slipping back into sleep. She slept peacefully and I just sat on the end of her bed for what seemed like hours but it must have been only a few moments. I went down the stairs and walked out of the house full of noise and chattering people and I was gone. The following day Judith phoned to tell us that Freda had passed away in her sleep painlessly. In her wisdom Bett left me to my thoughts for the rest of the day. I think she sensed that I would need her to be near me over the following days. Two weeks after Freda passed away Bett and I were sitting out in the porch that overlooked our garden. It was January and the ground was covered in snow; the scene was entirely peaceful. Since Freda's death I had lived almost like a recluse, hardly speaking to anyone.

I said, 'You do know, Bett, that I will never let you down.'

'I know that, Vic. I also know that you've had a hard time with your thoughts.'

At last I had unloaded from my mind the events I had seen and done. The years of killing, the death of my friends, the genocide of Dresden. I unloaded the lot, along with the almost overpowering hate that I seemed unable to get rid of.

'That cup of hate, Bett, was full to the brim, and it spilled over on to the ones I loved. I hurt them all, and I have no excuses.'

Bett was not a woman for crying. Instead she disappeared into the kitchen and came out with a nice hot cup of tea.

'So, Vic, you've got it all off your chest at last, you wait and see, things will be better for you now.'

What I remember the most of the weeks that followed was that I spent a whole lot of time clearing out mementos of my past. I remember turning over a batch of spanners in a drawer in my shed and there, staring me in the face, was the pair of brass knuckledusters. I threw everything away and by the time I had satisfied myself that there was nothing but the future in the house I had filled two skips and a couple of dustbins.

We continued to live happily in South Wales until we were offered a flat in Winchester owned and run by the welfare office of my old regiment, the Rifle Brigade. We now have as neighbours men and their wives who have served their country in every corner of the globe, men, all of whom at some stage in their life, have had to put their head above the parapet and place their trust in their mates around them. I have done what I have done and got away with it by more luck than judgement. But I am an optimist, and what we learned in the army is as true of everyday life as it is of battle: if things are getting too hot, take a breather and brew up the tea. It will all come out in the wash.

EPILOGUE

It is now the autumn of 2015 and my life has almost run its course. My ninety-fifth birthday has come and gone and an event has just occurred that, had it happened many years ago, I might have lived my days in a much more civilised manner.

In early January of this year I received a letter from the Dean of Coventry, The Very Revd John Witcombe, MA MPhil, no less. He asked me if I could attend the seventy-fifth anniversary commemoration of the bombing of Dresden, an event to be held in the cathedral. I was stunned by this invitation, especially bearing in mind my antipathy towards religion of any sort. But I was aware that the cathedral and I had something in common: a desire for the complete reconciliation between the peoples of Germany and Britain. I accepted the Dean's invitation and said that I would cooperate in any way I could with his service.

I had many kind offers of help from people who thought that it might be difficult for a man of my age to make his own way from Winchester to Coventry but I wanted to visit the cathedral as an act of pilgrimage. I didn't want an easy journey, I wanted to attend in homage to the thousands of men, women and children whom I had watched enduring agony and suffering in the act of dying. Praying for lost souls was not part of my agenda. What I wanted was to remind people never to forget the horrors that man can impose on his fellows.

I duly turned up on a bright and very cold Sunday morning to be greeted by the church staff and the Dean who told me that I was to give a talk to the assembled congregation about why I was there and what the service meant to me. This was something I was not prepared for. I can't remember exactly what I said that day but for the first time in my life I stood up straight and faced nearly a thousand devout Christians and committed myself to telling the truth about the horrors I had witnessed and why I thought that what we had done in Dresden was wrong. I said that it would never be enough for people to attend their local church and offer up prayers to some god in the hope that he would somehow make us all loving and peaceful towards each other. I told the people gathered in the cathedral that they had to be prepared to lay their bodies in the road in order to stop the cannons reaching the firing line. I remember finishing and holding up my hands and there being silence. Then came a solitary clap and next, to my surprise, the congregation gave me a standing ovation. What I had said to earn this I honestly do not know. I knew that I had been talking for about twenty-five minutes. I was relieved that I had said nothing wrong and by some miracle all had gone down well.

At the end of the service a lot of people came up to wish me peace and love. What meant the most to me was when I was approached by an elderly lady who had tears in her eyes. She was German and as a young woman had lived with her family in Dresden. On the night of the bombing she had been visiting a friend away from the city centre. She told me she had lost her whole family in the raid. I placed my arms around her and we were bound together as one, joined in our memories of that awful night. I have to admit to being reduced to tears as we finally parted.

I have never before in my life experienced the feeling of love and common cause with another human being that I experienced with that elderly lady. One thing I am certain of is that if the episode had occurred sixty years earlier I might not have been the angry, violent man I became for all those years. I'm still not a believer but now, late in life though it may be, my mind is at peace, the devils and the nightmares will never return. Sharing those few moments with that lady gave me a new future. I bless her.

If by putting pen to paper I have played a part in bringing a halt to the idea that the killing of our fellow man can ever be justified, then the project can be considered to have been worthwhile. What more can a man ask as a requiem?

Victor Gregg
Swanmore, 2015

INDEX

ALSO AVAILABLE BY VICTOR GREGG

KING'S CROSS KID:
A CHILDHOOD BETWEEN THE WARS

The highly entertaining prequel to the same author's best-selling *Rifleman*

Ninety-three-year-old Victor Gregg has had a rich and fascinating life. *King's Cross Kid* follows his London childhood from the age of five, when life was so hard that the Salvation Army arranged for young Vic to be taken to the Shaftesbury Home for Destitute Children. Home again a year later, the scallywag years of late childhood began. Then, after the years of street gangs and run-ins with the law, Vic leaves school at fourteen and his real adventures start, and with them a working-class apprenticeship in survival. Ending with his enlistment in the army on the day of his eighteenth birthday, this prequel to the bestselling *Rifleman* will appeal to the many readers who were charmed by Victor Gregg's engaging, honest and warm voice.

'Intensely moving ****' Juliet Gardiner

'Evocative, detailed and unsentimental' David Kynaston

'One of the best first-hand accounts by a combat infantryman that I have read ... This gripping book immediately joins a select band of the best soldiers' stories told from the sharp end. It is a classic *****' *Mail on Sunday*

ORDER YOUR COPY:

BY PHONE: +44 (0) 1256 302 699; BY EMAIL: DIRECT@MACMILLAN.CO.UK

DELIVERY IS USUALLY 3–5 WORKING DAYS. FREE POSTAGE AND PACKAGING FOR ORDERS OVER £20.

ONLINE: WWW.BLOOMSBURY.COM/BOOKSHOP

PRICES AND AVAILABILITY SUBJECT TO CHANGE WITHOUT NOTICE.

WWW.BLOOMSBURY.COM/AUTHOR/VICTOR-GREGG/

BLOOMSBURY